Sunset storm over Mount Elbert (photo by Jon Kedrowski).

# Foreword

I've spent more than a few nights under the stars in my forty years of photographing nature. Though a tent is good shelter from wind, rain, and snow, I prefer being under the stars. I lie on my ThermaRest with my unzipped sleeping bag serving as a blanket, only tucking the edges under the inflatable pad when the wind picks up. Thusly covered, above the Colorado tree line and well into the alpine tundra, the views of the Milky Way on a moonless night allow my mind to go places it cannot under other circumstances. With no tree, no mountaintop within my peripheral vision, when I look up, all I can see is stars. On more than one occasion, I have felt as if I was on a spaceship racing through the universe, and have even experienced motion sickness as my imagination turned me into an astronaut.

Jon and Chris have done something I've thought about a lot, but never done: sleep on top of a Colorado Fourteener. Or sleep on fifty-four fourteeners. In ninety-five days. To climb that many peaks in so short a time is a magnificent physical and mental achievement that can only be accomplished by a focused and fit individual. To persevere nature's capriciousness, if not violence, on top of the world is an additional triumph. To survive summer's killer electrical storms in places synonymous with a lightning rod is almost a miracle. Thank goodness for Chris's weather-forecasting skills. Like Odysseus arriving home from the Trojan War after surviving ten years of mythological challenges in the *Odyssey*, so too would there be a reward for Jon's courage and resolve during his own odyssey.

There is no light like *mountain light*. When the sun sets and rises, physics changes white light to yellow, orange, red, and magenta. Summer monsoon rain intensifies the effect. After and before those events, when the monsoon has evaporated, twilight colors the sky with fuchsia, purple, royal blue, and eventually black, while red, orange, and yellow adhere to the horizon. It's sensory overload. And *magna cum overload* from 14,000 feet! Absolute silence … no birds, no gurgling creeks, no wind much of the time. The constant nip of cold on the cheeks … even when Denver is melting. Above all else, there's the sensuousness of *place*. And there are those stars, and thoughts of what lies out *there*. And questions in your mind of just what exactly is this thing … *there*. And if you're lucky while you're pondering big thoughts, you get motion sickness.

—JOHN FIELDER,
nature photographer

Jon and Chris on Mount Elbert, winter 2009.

# Preface

## CHASING A DREAM

We kept wondering when the next tent pole would break. Fifty mph wind gusts are not uncommon at 14,440 feet, and on that night we were feeling the jet stream. Just an hour earlier we had secured our four-season tent on the highest point in Colorado—the very summit of Mount Elbert.

We knew it was going to be a long night. Wind creates a deafening noise when it rattles your tent and blows debris against the fabric walls. Our heads were in a fog, as neither of us completely acclimatized to the altitude on that winter's eve. We rambled about future projects, which is something we do regularly—Jon and I are big dreamers. This foray to the top of Colorado was merely a training exercise for Jon's upcoming trip to Denali later that spring.

The idea of sleeping on every Colorado Fourteener (14er) summit came up numerous times that long night. It had never been done. We wondered if it was possible to carry overnight gear to the top of every 14er, avoid bad weather, stay the night from sunset to sunrise, and live to tell the tale. We knew from experience that there was room for a tent on nearly all the summits, even though some summits are only the size of a family dinner table. I knew that I wouldn't be able to do every 14er because of work, but I'd be monitoring the weather for Jon.

Nearly 750,000 people every year attempt to climb a Colorado 14er. Ninety-nine percent of those attempts are done with an "alpine start" in the months of July, August, and September. An alpine start is a predawn start that gets you to the summit and then down the mountain before the afternoon thunderstorms develop. The objective is to reach the summit and descend before lightning moves in. For our dream to succeed, we'd be climbing the 14ers at the worst possible time of the day—right in the middle of the afternoon thunderstorms, not to mention the seasonal monsoon. To make each summit in time for sunset, our weather forecasting skills would have to be impeccable. Extra moisture floods the atmosphere above Colorado in July and August, making afternoon monsoon thunderstorms more likely, more wet, and more violent. Oftentimes these storms can last well into the night. We'd need to avoid having a late-night lightning storm sneak in while we slept.

That night on Mount Elbert our dream was born. We would continue planning the fine details of this endeavor in the months ahead. This book is largely about teamwork. It's about taking risks and climbing the preverbal mountain to see what you're made of. It's meant to inspire, motivate, and is proof that anything is possible.

## WHERE GEOGRAPHY AND METEOROLOGY COLLIDE

Over a period of ninety-five days, from June 23 to September 28, 2011, Jon spent his entire summer climbing to the summit of the 58 highest peaks in Colorado (all exceeding 14,000 feet) while sleeping on the summit of most of them from sunset to sunrise. "Bivouac" is a term first used by French climbers in the Alps. The term refers to "a long night of suffering," and Jon did just that for nearly sixty nights on his way to completing this project. But, there was a lot more to this adventure than suffering. When I wasn't on a summit with Jon, I supplied the weather forecasts via phone and

text messages. All told for the Sierra Designs–sponsored project, Kedrowski spent complete nights on fifty-four "official" 14er peaks, and four "naps" on unofficial 14er peaks. To be an "official" 14er, a summit needs to have at least 300 feet of prominence (elevation), and these measurements have changed over time with improved measuring devices. The U.S. Geological Survey (USGS) has also named more than 54 summits in Colorado over 14,000 feet, and so it was decided that a few additional peaks including both Maroon Bells and El Diente should be slept on as well. Jon also found time to travel to Washington state for a brief trip to guide friends up Mount Rainier (14,411 feet) for the third year in a row. There, he also spent the night on the summit of that highest peak in Washington.

Our motto is "speed is safety" in the mountains. We travel light and fast. It's almost as if we've been prepping for years just to complete this project. It's possible to replace gear with knowledge, creating a lighter pack, and the knowledge making this project possible consisted of Jon's background in mountain geography and my knowledge of mountain meteorology. Jon's a Ph.D. mountain geographer and I'm a bonafide meteorologist. It's classic teamwork. We trust each other's judgment and know each other's strengths and weaknesses.

We've both climbed all of the fourteeners by various routes in all seasons. Knowing the terrain, escape routes, and travel times was part and parcel to our success.

## The Rooftop of Colorado: The Geography of Mountain Meteorology

Weather can make or break a trip into the mountains. During the summer months the weather warms up and the winds calm at 14,000 feet. June to September represents the warmest window for hiking in Colorado's high country. Jon's research shows that most 14ers are climbed in July, August, and September. It can snow any month of the year on a 14er, but July and August represent your best shot at making a snow-free 14er summit.

During the winter months, the jet stream descends to the top of the 14ers. This superhighway of wind is created by temperature differences across North America. The jet stream contains 200 mph wind speeds and helps guide cold fronts and storms around the country. Colorado is a battleground in the winter, with cold fronts arriving every few days. It's extremely difficult to climb a 14er in the winter and not experience high winds.

During the summer months the jet stream moves away from the 14ers. Lighter winds prevail and significantly fewer cold fronts slide through Colorado. After the high peaks lose their snow, daily afternoon thunderstorms begin to develop. These storms grow as the sun heats the mountains, and that air rises, condenses, and clouds develop. It's a pattern that repeats itself almost every day of the summer. Some days these storms develop earlier and some days later, but the rule of thumb is to get off a 14er summit by noon.

Monsoon season is a special case. During July and August, new moisture flows into Colorado from the south and southwest. This moisture acts as fuel, accelerating afternoon thunderstorm development. It also makes storms wetter, more frequent, and more violent. Lightning is the number one weather killer in Colorado. During monsoon season, thunderstorms can develop earlier in the day and last well into the night. As a result, special caution needs to be taken during July and August.

—Chris Tomer

Storm over Capitol Peak.

# Fourteener Locations

## San Juan Mountains

2. Wetterhorn Peak
3. San Luis Peak
4. Handies Peak
5. Uncompahgre Peak
6. Redcloud Peak
7. Sunshine Peak
8. Mount Eolus
9. North Eolus
10. Sunlight Peak
11. Windom Peak
12. Mount Wilson
13. Wilson Peak
14. El Diente Peak
15. Mount Sneffels

## Ten Mile and Mosquito Range

16. Mount Cameron
17. Mount Lincoln
18. Mount Democrat
19. Mount Bross
20. Quandary Peak
21. Mount Sherman

## Elk Mountains

22. Castle Peak
23. Conundrum Peak
24. Maroon Peak
25. North Maroon Peak
26. Pyramid Peak
27. Snowmass Mountain
28. Capitol Peak

## Front Range

29. Mount Bierstadt
30. Grays Peak
31. Mount Evans
32. Torreys Peak
33. Longs Peak
34. Pikes Peak

## Sangre de Cristo Range

35. Ellingwood Point
36. Blanca Peak
37. Mount Lindsey
38. Culebra Peak
39. Little Bear Peak
40. Crestone Peak
41. Crestone Needle
42. Humboldt Peak
43. Challenger Point
44. Kit Carson Peak

## Sawatch Range

1. La Plata Peak
45. Mount Elbert
46. Huron Peak
47. Missouri Mountain
48. Mount Oxford
49. Mount Belford
50. Mount Shavano
51. Tabeguache Peak
52. Mount Antero
53. Mount Princeton
54. Mount Harvard
55. Mount Columbia
56. Mount Yale
57. Mount Massive
58. Mount of the Holy Cross

Note: Numbers indicate mountain location, not the order that summits were completed. Chronological order of summits climbed and camped on can be found in Appendix A.

Denver

Map data available from U.S. Geological Survey, DEMs produced by Matthew Novak, hillshades by Jon Kedrowski

# Introduction

COLORADO FOURTEENERS: ICONS

Dr. Jon Kedrowski based his Master's Thesis on the climbing frequency of Colorado's Fourteeners, and has followed up that research for the better part of the last decade with numerous trail assessments and research articles on the peaks. According to his research, over 750,000 people attempt to climb a 14er every year. It's a staggering number, and a number that, according to Jon, continues to grow annually—up from 200,000 in the late 1990s. The economic impact of just one climber is significant—climbers stay in hotels, eat at restaurants, and buy gasoline.

The most-climbed 14er in Colorado is Longs Peak, located in Rocky Mountain National Park (RMNP). The data shows that over 10,000 attempts are made on Longs summit every year. Longs Peak is not a beginner's peak, but because of its location within RMNP it is often treated as such. Numerous deaths have been recorded on Longs. It's an arduous sixteen-mile round-trip climb through various kinds of terrain. Summertime thunderstorms can quickly turn parts of Longs into a death trap. It's a race against the weather and other climbers.

Jon's research indicates that the most-climbed 14ers are all located near the Front Range of Colorado. This is the population epicenter of the state. These 14ers are easily accessed and rarely require an overnight camp. Three hundred hikers or more routinely stand together on the summit of Grays Peak on a July Saturday. Recent attempts to maintain trails have been very problematic due to climber impact and erosion, and recent funding allocation for new trails appears unequally distributed. Case in point—the Maroon Bells, where over $300,000 has been allocated by the Colorado Fourteeners Initiative (CFI), but ironically fewer than three hundred people per year attempt these peaks. The numbers just don't add up. Funding should be allocated more toward peaks that have higher use levels, and the actual routes leading to many of the very difficult 14ers still don't see enough climbers to warrant building trails over very steep and marginally unstable terrain.

The most isolated 14ers are located in the San Juan Mountains, located in southwestern Colorado. In particular, the Needle Range contains three 14ers requiring a long backpack, and is often paired with a ride on the Durango Narrow Gauge Railroad. Eolus, Sunlight, and Windom peaks are located in the Chicago Basin, buried deep within the Needle Range. Summiting these three peaks together normally demands two to three overnights. However, their isolation is also an attraction. An unprecedented number of climbers (up to 100,000 per year) now venture into the Chicago Basin.

The most challenging and dangerous 14ers in Colorado include Capitol Peak, Little Bear Peak, Mount Wilson, El Diente, Maroon Bells, and the Crestones. The most difficult 14ers are also weather magnets. Get a feel for how storms build around these peaks before attempting to climb them. This project demonstrates that all of these jagged peaks are shaped by the unique geology and natural erosional forces of Colorado's harsh weather and climate.

"On additional climbing trips, we just couldn't stop talking about the possibility of camping on the top of every single mountain," recalls Kedrowski. "Since we had both climbed all of Colorado's 14ers, and knew a great deal about the physical geography as well as the weather and climate of the peaks, we thought that this challenging project would be a great way to not only contribute to the history of the 14ers, but to see if sleeping on every summit was even possible. In short, it would be a great test of teamwork in the mountains, and Chris and I knew we could help each other accomplish this feat."

Early morning in the Elk Mountains.

Chris on Sneffels.

Trying to find the best way to document the project, we decided to organize this book by mountain range, therefore the climbs and corresponding summit bivys are not listed consecutively in some places. Each chapter is a mountain range and each mountain range has the summit bivys listed in the order they were done. The story follows this general format. Most of the time the goal was to try and climb all the peaks in one range together. This didn't always happen, but most of the time it did. Weather, geographic location, and many other factors that played into this amazing journey determined to a certain degree the order in which each peak's summit was slept on. The climbs are listed in consecutive order in Appendix A.

## SLEEPING ON THE SUMMIT OF A COLORADO FOURTEENER: ESSENTIALS TO CONSIDER

Do you want to sleep on a fourteener summit? Here's what we learned after sleeping on them all.

*The most important variable to consider is the weather.* Before packing a single bag, be sure you understand the weather forecast inside and out. Equally as important, educate yourself on mountain meteorology. Being able to diagnose the weather you see unfolding in the field can save your life. This kind of knowledge will help you decide whether to attack the summit or turn around and go home. Consult local weather experts for information, or attend personalized mountain meteorology workshops. Just getting the feel for the flow of weather systems in Colorado takes years—go out and learn by climbing as many peaks as you can!

*Know the mountain geography, and specifically the route topography.* Research the peak and know the escape routes if bad weather rolls in. Know where the last possible water stops are to lighten your load. Knowing the route will also give you a good estimate of how long it will take you to reach the summit. Keep in mind you'll be carrying overnight gear and will only be as fast as your heaviest pack and slowest group member.

*Increase your fitness and acclimatization ahead of time.* Efficiency is a key piece of the puzzle, and if you're in great shape you feel better and can move faster. Sleep on a 12,000- or 13,000-footer first to get acclimatized. If a dangerous storm moves in, you'll need to have the speed to escape.

*Lighten your load.* The more weight you carry the slower you will move. Heavy weight also increases fatigue. We were bare-minimalists during this project, so you'll have to experiment to see what you can survive without. We found the essentials to be a 15-degree down ultralight sleeping bag, pad, ultralight two-person tent, one ultralight bivy sack, an ultralight hoody down jacket, a rain jacket and rain pants, water reservoir, headlamp, energy bars, hat, gloves, cameras, sunscreen, sunglasses, toilet paper, ultraviolet water purifier, and pre-packaged pizza. We didn't bring stoves. Hot food and hot beverages are luxuries for weekends at the lake with friends. On a few of the multi-day 14ers, Jon carried a stove, but it was a very small and light MSR Pocket-Rocket.

*Know your limits.* You should climb a 14er in traditional alpine style before attempting an overnight bivy. Start easy and build from there—you might find that it's one of the most difficult things you've ever done. The Front Range is full of 14ers that are good testpieces. Good luck and be safe out there on your adventures!

# La Plata Peak
## The Start of an Incredible Journey

**14,336 feet** (39° 01' 46" N; 106° 28' 23" W)
**Bivy** June 23–24

## Inspired by Firsts

La Plata was the first peak of this project. By 7:00 p.m. we were resting in our separate tents admiring the view across the top of Colorado. We made quick work of La Plata's southwest ridge from Winfield in less than three hours with overnight gear. We traveled fast and light—a strategy we've practiced for years in the mountains. I set up my tent on La Plata's highest point behind a small rock shelter and we threw on our down jackets as the sun began to set. Chris set up twenty yards away on the ridge. There was hardly any wind.

"La Plata" means silver in Spanish, and the peak was so named by prospectors that first came to the area and found silver among the dark greyish-brown and streaky 1.7-billion-year-old granite. Most of the peak's silver is the direct result of the cooling of magma within the 65-million-year-old igneous intrusion known as the Twin Lakes Batholith. Perhaps the old prospectors were inspired enough by their valuable discoveries in the 1870s to climb this peak and take in the views.

Opposite: Sunset on Day One. Above: Looking south into Winfield Basin and Sayres Peak (13,738 feet) en route to the first bivy.
Left: Chris and his tent illuminated by the sunset.

A windy morning on La Plata, one down, fifty-seven to go.

**Meteorology  Chris:** La Plata Peak sits in the heart of the tallest peaks in Colorado. During the summer months, afternoon thunderstorms develop like clockwork above La Plata and across all the surrounding mountain ranges, including the Elks, Sawatch, Sangres, and the San Juans to the southwest. Once these storms reach maturity, the prevailing wind will push them in various directions. It's critical to note the direction of the prevailing wind. It's possible to get hit with storms early in the afternoon and again later in the evening, as storms that may have developed over the Elks or even the San Juans push east-northeast with the prevailing wind.

Because of its location, La Plata Peak is a lightning magnet. Lightning from distant storms can still kill you. For example, if you see lightning or hear thunder that may be occurring on nearby peaks such as Elbert, Huron, or even the Belford Group, it's a good idea to descend.

Luckily, our night on La Plata Peak was storm-free. The July-August monsoon had not yet engaged.

## Driven from Within by the Views and the Task Ahead

Chris and I were snapping photos of a beautiful sunset—a sight very few people ever get to witness at over 14,000 feet. While impressive, it was also a daunting sight. Could this effort be repeated over fifty more times? Camping on every Colorado Fourteener summit had never been done before, but I was determined to try. I was driven to succeed, and Chris was there to support my journey every step of the way. It takes some people a lifetime to climb all of the Fourteener peaks, let alone trying to do them all in one summer and spend the night on every single one from sunset to sunrise.

The summit of this first bivy was an excellent vantage point. La Plata Peak is very unique because you can see all six major Colorado mountain ranges: Front Range to Pikes Peak; Tenmile Range to Lincoln and Democrat; southeast to the Sangres and the Crestones; west to the Elks and the tons of snow on the Maroon Bells, Castle, Snowmass, and Capitol; and clear to Uncompaghre in the San Juans. The remainder of the Sawatch Range was in the foreground to the north and south.

Back in my tent, in the comfort of my warm sleeping bag, I began jotting down my thoughts:
"We are in the center of it all, the focal point to which this project could become very special, where we could make history. I am sitting near the roof of Colorado and have set a monumental goal. I see it layed out in front of me, all of the peaks in all their beauty, danger, and glory. I feel inspired and want to transcend greatness and do something that has never been done before. There will be lots of sunny days, plenty of windy ones, a few scary moments, some stormy weather, and some incredible triumphs. There will be lots of stories to tell and a lifetime of memories. I'm ready for the challenge and excited about the journey, it's going to be a very special ride."

—Excerpt from Jon's bivys project journal, Thursday, June 23, 2011

Link to video of each summit with your smart phone.

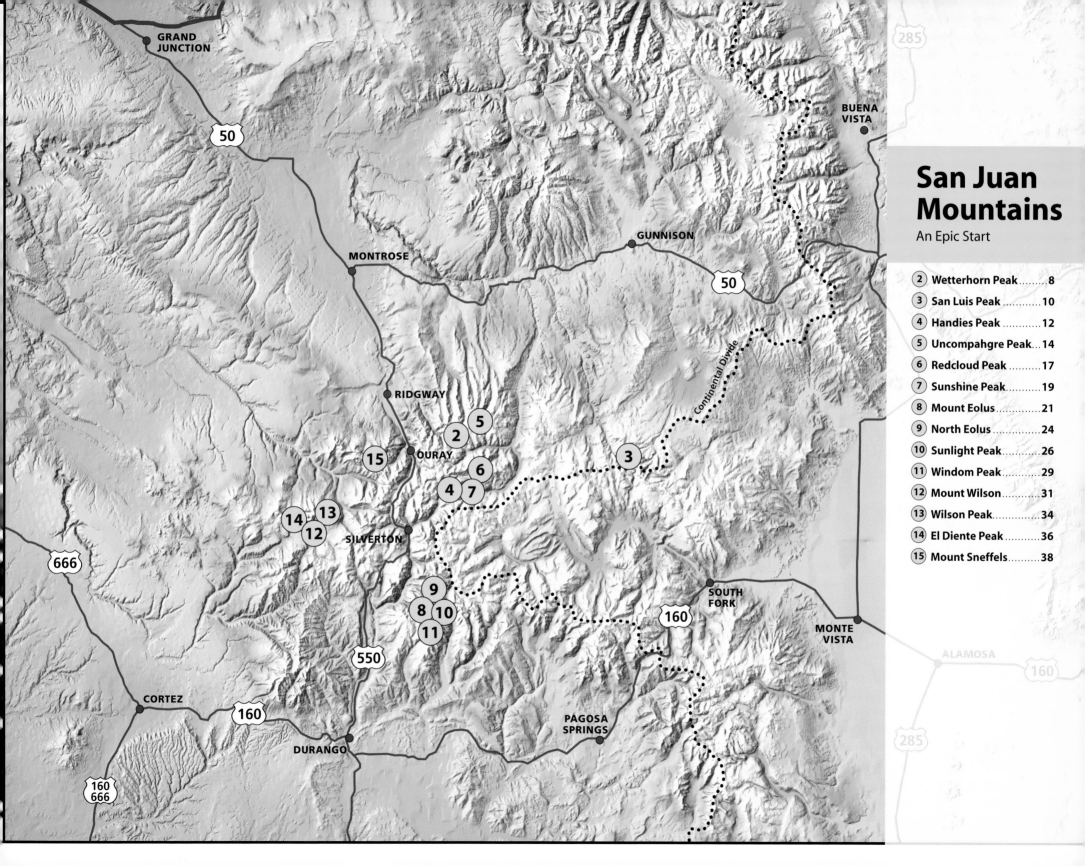

# San Juan Mountains

An Epic Start

# Wetterhorn
# Peak Weather Peak

**14,015 feet** (38° 3' 38" N; 107° 30' 39" W)
**Bivy** June 27–28

# "Wetting" My 14er Appetite

I had a feeling that this project wasn't going to be easy. Knowing that the San Juans are a difficult range and so far away from my home base in Vail, I decided to head there early in the project. I was amazed in 2005 when I climbed sixty-two Colorado 14ers in forty-two days and also Elbrus (Europe's highest peak) in Russia as well, without getting any type of sicknesses whatsoever. So here I am, sitting at the Lake City Resort after quite a challenging ordeal in the past twenty-four hours to say the least. I rented a small cabin with a kitchenette, made some dinner, and got a hot shower to restore my spirits and my energy. Not terribly resorty if you ask me, but a much needed recovery period after what I experienced on Wetterhorn.

As the sun began to set last night, I boiled water for my dinner and hot drinks and took plenty of sunset photos—the vast expanse of the San Juans dominated the views in all directions. To the south and west these high peaks were still buried in a thick mantle of snow. To the north and east you could see all the way to the Elk and Sawatch Ranges, and to the northwest to Grand Mesa and the Grand Junction valley.

The entire San Juan range was part of a giant super-volcano known as the "San Juan Dome," which erupted and later collapsed into a series of large calderas, or craters, roughly 28 to 30 million years ago. Wetterhorn's relatively small summit block and exciting summit pitch (pictured right) is the most resistant of the grey-brown, and even red ash-flow tuff. This resistance is the reason why the summit is very flat, small, and difficult to climb to, with cliffs guarding all sides of the top. Layers near the 14,000-foot elevation have weathered away almost completely, leaving the last bit of only the most time-tested rock from the Ute Creek Caldera.

Opposite: Looking east, the setting sun illuminates the top of Colorado's Matterhorn (center right), with Uncompahgre in the distance.

Top: Sunset.

Above: Wetterhorn's snowy southeast face.

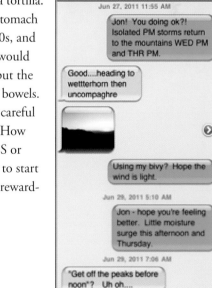

# The Perfect Omelet Gone Wrong

I was eating my dinner—an omelet of eggs, onion, and green pepper wrapped in a tortilla. I was pretty hungry, so it went down easy. But when I went to bed, it suddenly happened. I couldn't get comfortable, my stomach started to hurt, and I got a headache, so I quickly reached for my stove to boil more water. Temperatures were in the 30s, and I felt like maybe it was just a little AMS (acute mountain sickness), so boiling water and drinking some hot chocolate would do the trick. I soon had water boiled and mixed up some hot chocolate. I took one sip and I couldn't stomach it, so I put the hot cup aside and tried to get comfortable. I dozed off for about forty-five minutes, when I was rudely awakened by my bowels. I had to go, and I had to go NOW! I quickly squirmed out of my tent, slipped shoes on, and ran down the hill (being careful not to slip off the cliff of the summit plateau). How could this be? Why was I getting sick with AMS or maybe a little food poisoning? Not a great way to start this project. Yep, it was going to be a long and rewarding summer!

**Meteorology** The weather pattern in the San Juans is dominated by the monsoon in July and August. However, that day on Wetterhorn was incredibly clear—one of those bluebird days high on a Colorado summit where there wasn't a whole lot to worry about regarding the afternoon storms. After all, it was still June, so the summer monsoon hadn't kicked in fully just yet.

Jon Kedrowski

Jun 27, 2011 11:55 AM

Jon! You doing ok?! Isolated PM storms return to the mountains WED PM and THR PM.

Good....heading to wetterhorn then uncompaghre

Using my bivy? Hope the wind is light.

Jun 29, 2011 5:10 AM

Jon - hope you're feeling better. Little moisture surge this afternoon and Thursday.

Jun 29, 2011 7:06 AM

"Get off the peaks before noon"? Uh oh....

# San Luis Peak Isolation Peak

**14,014 feet** (37° 59' 12" N; 106° 55' 53" W)
**Bivy** June 29–30

Above: Sunset.                    Right: Sunrise.

Left: San Luis from the southwest.

Below: Following the Colorado Trail to reach the south ridge.

## Isolation in the La Garita Wilderness

San Luis is one of Colorado's most remote and least-climbed fourteener. It is the San Juan's easternmost 14,000-foot peak, situated in a lost corner of Colorado in a sub-range of the San Juan Mountains known as the La Garita Range.

In 2005, I had my very first experience with lightning on San Luis while climbing fourteeners. I chose to continue up the east ridge of San Luis without being able to see the weather coming from the west. Needless to say, I felt charges, my jacket zippers were buzzing, and my hair was standing up as I sprinted off the summit following a trail evaluation for a project I was working on.

I hadn't been back to San Luis in six years, so I opted for the south ridge of the peak for the summit bivy access via the Colorado Trail, and I wasn't disappointed.

## A "Tuff" Night in High Winds

It was no surprise that along the Colorado Trail that afternoon, I had to patiently wait out a strong lightning storm. By 5:00 p.m. it had quickly passed over and I felt confident I could tag the summit and get set up before sunset. For the last 500 feet of the south ridge, the winds were howling—sustaining 40 mph for the rest of the evening and all night. Fortunately, storms were staying south and east of San Luis as the sun set below overcast skies. I knew it would be safe to stay the night.

Once on the broad and flat summit, I took advantage of the dark lava, grey ash tuff, and mud flow breccia rock, including some of the granite and porphyry blocks to build up a nice windbreak for the tent. These rocks near the summit of San Luis were placed here nearly 27 million years ago when the "Nelson Mountain" volcano just to the east of San Luis collapsed and formed a large caldera, leaving these dark volcanic remnants behind.

**Meteorology** The lightning storms are especially common on San Luis because of its location on the northeast periphery of the San Juan Mountains. Storms that develop over the San Juans in summer usually track from southwest to northeast, and this track delivers a direct hit on San Luis Peak, packing a powerful punch with up-draft winds and dangerous lightning. The ascending ridges to the summit are long, so exposure above timberline is sustained during the summit trek.

# Handies
# Peak
### Deep in the Heart of the San Juans

**14,048 feet** (37° 54' 47" N; 107° 30' 16" W)
**Bivy** June 30–July 1

## Mountains as Far as the Eye Can See

Getting down from San Luis peak earlier in the day, I grabbed lunch in Lake City and headed up to American Basin. It was rainy and turbulent up high that afternoon as I ascended the 4WD road up into the basin, watching lightning and hearing the thunder crackle across the vast wilderness. As I parked my truck in the lower reaches of American Basin, the rain and hail came down in sheets from 3:00 to 4:30 p.m. Chris had indicated the weather would clear as the entire storm system rolled east, so I waited out the storm.

At five o'clock, I loaded up my pack with food and water for the night, and took the well-worn American Basin Trail up the

Left: Early morning alpenglow. Top: Sunset.
Above: Sunrise looking southwest.

Clear and windy on the southwest slopes, following the well-worn trail to the summit.

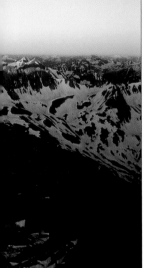

standard route to the west slopes and ridge of Handies Peak. Winds were still strong up above timberline, but I covered up and reached the summit by 6:30 p.m. I had plenty of time to set up my tent—in strong winds for the second night in a row—with stunning views of mountains in all directions.

## The San Juan Volcanic Dome

Handies has a relatively flat summit along a steep-sided ridge with a large cornice remaining by July (at least in 2011), and steep drop-offs to the east. Only a few rocks were piled on the summit, the cap being mainly green-grey sandstone, and a grey lava flow.

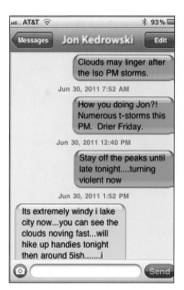

**Meteorology** On that day, a large high-pressure center moved eastward along the Colorado–New Mexico border. The system was exiting the region by late afternoon but continued to push moisture up from the south. Once the moisture and rain cleared, due to a dry continental air mass to the west, the storms stopped, but the wrap-around impacts from the clockwise center of rotation in the high-pressure system continued to pound the peak with winds that stayed 30 to 40 mph all night long.

**Chris:** The dominant weather pattern was simply the development of afternoon thunderstorms—some of them strong. Prevailing winds were strong enough to push these storms east of Handies by late afternoon. Skies cleared that night for Jon but the winds remained stiff. I highly recommend avoiding San Juan 14ers during the heart of monsoon season, at least after high noon. Most days in July and August feature violent thunderstorms.

I quickly built a small shelter of rocks to block the wind from the west and set up my tent perpendicular to the wind, with my tent door facing east. The San Juan Dome, also known as the Uncompaghre Caldera, collapsed nearly 30 million years ago, leaving behind red-to-brown tuff, breccia, and lava ash flow, especially distinct on lower reaches of the mountain, and also portions of the San Juan Mountains extending north and west of Handies' summit, as the ancient caldera came after the up-lifting volcanic dome of the San Juans.

After boiling some water, I went to bed. This was my third fourteener summit in four nights, and I felt the best I had felt on the project to date. My body was starting to acclimatize to the nights above 14,000 feet. I slept most of the night before my customary 5:30 a.m. rising to get sunrise photos. I woke to a perfectly clear morning, surrounded by peaks upon peaks!

# Uncompahgre
# Peak Incomparably Red

**14,309 feet** (38° 04' 18" N; 107° 27' 44" W)
**Bivy** July 1–2

### Highest Bivy in the San Juans

The Nellie Creek Basin was quiet and calm. I was ascending the highest peak in the San Juan Mountains, hoping Chris didn't see anything tracking my way on radar. Meanwhile, thirty-five miles to the east, a series of afternoon thunderstorms were unleashing their fury on San Luis Peak, and I was grateful that I had already been up there forty-eight hours earlier. I could tell by their movement that those storms weren't coming in my direction.

As I quickly made my way up toward the ridgeline, the views became outstanding. Climbing this peak on a warm summer afternoon was definitely the way to go. Once I gained the summit plateau, I was reassured the evening would be clear by scanning the western sky. The contrast between storms to the east and clear to the west was an excellent recipe for a sunset spectacular.

Top: Upper Nellie Creek Basin. Above: Summit camp and mountain pyramid shadow.

Opposite: Uncompahgre's flat summit and a 2,000-foot drop off the north face.

Top: Sunset on Uncompahgre with Wetterhorn to the southwest, just above the tent in the distance.

Above: A heavily used trail leading to Uncompahgre from the standard Nellie Creek Basin approach.

## Rocks that Make Water Red

The Ute Indians were probably the first to ascend to Uncompahgre's vast summit while hunting wildlife in the basins below. They may have even been the first to spend the night up on this large summit plateau, steep on all sides, but providing an excellent vantage point to observe the migration of elk herds below.

It was here that the Ute word Uncompahgre was derived. The Utes noticed the crystal clear water, sometimes tinted reddish-brown from bright red lava and breccia rocks, including the layer of sandstone capping the summit plateau. The rim of the ancient Uncompahgre Caldera passes just north of the peak and is visible on some of the ridges in the distance. Best of all, the nearly two thousand-foot drop off the north face of the peak was quite a sight, and more than once during the night you could hear the howl and echoes of the coyotes down in the basin. Perched right near the edge of the cliff, I had to remember not to venture too far from the tent. I had company on the summit that night—a gold and grey fox was also sheltering among the red boulders.

**Meteorology** The start of July is still pre-monsoon season, so thunderstorms in the afternoon aren't as strong just yet, and they can be hit-or-miss. Because Uncompahgre is much higher than the surrounding mountains, it provided a stellar "pyramid" shadow as the sun set among the storms to the east, a real treat. Fortunately the winds were light that evening, but the peak can certainly have high winds since it rises so high above the surrounding landscape.

# Redcloud Peak Deep Red

**14,034 feet** (37° 56' 27" N; 107° 25' 17" W)
**Bivy** July 2–3

**Meteorology** The clash between an oncoming monsoon and fronts coming from the north and west can often lead to long and stable weather windows during early July. A prevailing front earlier in the week pushed through, pulling some moisture up into the San Juans from the south, hence the hit-or-miss thunderstorms. Once the system had passed through, more of a drier continental westerly and even northwesterly flow dominated and kept the afternoons dry. This made for a great opportunity to stay up on the high ridges all day long.

Tomer recalls the weather pattern on Sunshine and Redcloud Peaks: "I wasn't worried about Jon at all on either Redcloud or Sunshine. The monsoon had yet to grab hold and the normal development of afternoon thunderstorms appeared to be minimal, if at all. Dry pockets of air had settled over most of the San Juans."

Northwesterly flows usually cease by mid-July when the monsoon fully takes over. Take advantage of Colorado Fourteeners and the weather by climbing prior to mid-July, and you will be rewarded. Just be ready and carry the appropriate footwear to handle the extra snow on the peaks.

Right: Martian-like soils on Redcloud's summit. Sunshine's distinct summit pyramid can be seen (center).

## First "Two-fer" of the Project

I was hoping the weather would stay on my side. For the last four peaks in the past five days I had reasonable weather, but more importantly, weather timing was on my side. I had waited out storms in some basins, and successfully spent the night on Wetterhorn, San Luis, Uncompahgre, and Handies. With a restful holiday weekend not far off, I needed to push through Redcloud and Sunshine, which lay ahead. Would the weather hold? I was betting it would and Chris reassured me.

Most people climb Redcloud and Sunshine together in a day from the Silver Creek–Grizzly Gulch trailhead. I decided to tackle the two peaks in a two-night backpack, which would put me up in the danger zone above the timber for more than thirty-six hours. I opted for the Mill Creek approach and climbed up and over Sunshine from the southeast and continued on to Redcloud after leaving my tent on Sunshine's summit.

## Oxidized Summit Soils

A light breeze was drifting in from the west, but there were no storms that evening. The soils on Redcloud are an even brighter red than Uncompahgre. Rich iron deposits within the rocks have oxidized in chemical reactions to stain these rocks (and my bivy sack) into brilliant reds. Although a tent could easily fit on the summit, I decided to take advantage of the perfect conditions and build a small wall and windbreak out of the granite, porphyry, tuff, and breccia rocks that coated the summit. Once my pad and bivy sack were set up, I boiled some water by melting the snow collected just feet from the summit and took in the calm sunset and crisp Colorado night under the stars.

Above: Morning light during the open bivy.

Right: Multiple trails lead south from Redcloud, seen here from the slopes of Sunshine.

# Sunshine Peak Lowest Fourteener

**14,001 feet** (37° 55' 22" N; 107° 25' 22" W)
**Bivy** July 3–4

## Barely a Fourteener—Should It be Counted?

Toss one rock off the top of Sunshine, and it's no longer considered a fourteener. I chose the east ridge of Sunshine via Mill Creek campground, a very steep and demanding climb and a 5,000-foot vertical gain to the summit. I made it in about three hours with a heavy pack from 1:00 to 4:00 p.m. on Saturday afternoon.

I set up my tent on Sunshine, in the very warm afternoon sunshine, and took a three-hour nap on the peak. Then, because Redcloud is the higher of the two sister peaks, I took my bivy sack over to the summit of Redcloud at 7:30 p.m. and slept there for the night, returning over to Sunshine in the morning for breakfast.

Sunrise on Sunshine.

## Youngest Fourteener, Excellent Guest Bedroom

I couldn't help but feel guilty up on Sunshine that morning after hiking over from Redcloud. I was about to take the tent down, but received another stellar forecast from Chris. Every peak had to be done, and although I was tired from five peaks in six days, I had to stay up on this one. The monsoon was going to hold off for another day, and I could still get down early the next day to visit family and friends to celebrate the Fourth of July. With no winds and bright blue skies, I literally took advantage of the sunshine and the amazing weather window.

Previous page: Looking north, Redcloud Peak is seen from Sunshine's summit. Uncompahgre Peak is on the horizon at the center of the photo.

Below: Sunshine's gentle north ridge.

Tuff and landslide breccia, including the piles of granite regolith made for an excellent recliner as I settled in for the day and thoroughly enjoyed the views and a book all day long. These rocks are the youngest in Colorado, only dating back 23 million years or so. The Lake City Caldera, one of the final collapses of volcanic activity in the San Juans, is seen just to the south of Sunshine. This region is not considered volcanically active today, and neither were the storms that afternoon.

**Meteorology** In the case of Sunshine, I had left my tent up on the summit, spent the previous night on Redcloud in the open, and then was already back to Sunshine by 8:00 a.m.. I ended up staying on that summit all day and was a potential "sitting duck." This happened a handful of times during the project, but I always had an escape plan and my pack ready to go at a moment's notice. If necessary, I could call Chris and get him to confirm storms and directional flow of cloud systems based on what I was seeing to help me decide if staying was safe or not. Fortunately the weather stayed perfect, further confirming the name of this fourteener.

The most difficult part of this project was worrying about the weather when there was a set of peaks to complete. Usually I would time my ascents to be on the individual summits by between 6:00 and 8:00 p.m., and then be off the summits by 7:00 a.m. after sunrise photos, thus minimizing time and risk up high. On Redcloud and Sunshine I had braved more than an entire day above 13,500 feet, including traversing from one peak to the next, and was happy the weather had let me stay.

# Mount Eolus On the Catwalk

**14,083 feet** (37° 37' 18" N; 107° 37' 22" W)
**Bivy** July 7–8

# Needle Mountain Adventures

I rode the Durango & Silverton Narrow Gauge Railroad to the Needleton trailhead, departing at 9:15 a.m. on a very warm summer morning in Durango. There were lots of tourists on the train, but only a few backpacks in the boxcar for people that were going to be dropped off at Needleton. In fact, at noon when we were dropped off, it was only me and one other couple.

I made quick work of the Needle Creek Trail, leaving the train and the Animas River Valley behind. Clouds were already building by 1:00 p.m., and I hiked through intermittent rain showers and occasional thunder, taking breaks here and there. I finally reached Chicago Basin and the upper basin of tree line by about 3:00 p.m. Off to the southwest you could see more clouds and hear thunder, so I dropped my pack, took cover under some trees, and cooked an early dinner. There was an incentive to eat my food—it would lighten the load in my pack. My pack was heavy by personal standards, so I decided to jettison some weight. I emptied out some clothes and a few food items, and hung

Top: Sunrise. Above: The Catwalk on Eolus. The Class 4 variation follows the ridge crest to the summit.

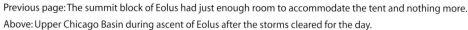

Previous page: The summit block of Eolus had just enough room to accommodate the tent and nothing more.

Above: Upper Chicago Basin during ascent of Eolus after the storms cleared for the day.

the extra weight in a tree. I would come back and get it later or in an emergency. I was packed for three peaks in three consecutive nights, and was hoping the weather would cooperate. Now that I had my pack to a manageable weight and the extra gear cached, I followed the cardinal rule of mountaineering: never get separated from your pack.

## God of Wind, or None at All

From 3:30 to 5:00 p.m. it thundered, poured rain, and looked nasty up high. The Greek God of Wind (Aeolus) was unleashing his full fury on the Needle Mountains. At about 5:15 p.m. I made a decision. I would take both the bivy sack and my tent and go up Eolus. I was confident that most of the afternoon thunderstorms were losing their strength and it was now or never. Cell service in the Needles was not happening, at least for that day, so I had to go with my gut, and my gamble paid off. I was up to Twin Lakes in the Chicago Basin at 12,100 feet by about 6:00 p.m., and then headed straight toward Eolus with the setting sun warming me and the mountain calling my name.

The Catwalk is maybe a Class 2+ (see Appendix B), but delightfully solid on grey and pink granite and feldspar crystals, making it easy to walk across. There are 500-foot drop-offs on either side. Once safely across, I made my way up the northeast ridge and did a fun Class 4 variation of the standard route, avoiding the east face and staying on the northeast ridge proper. The summit was mine in the waning evening sun by about 7:30 p.m.! Storms had cleared and there was no wind at all.

Eolus is an interesting summit. Not much room for a tent except on the summit block. I set up my tent on the 20-degree sloping granite block and proceeded to get some awesome and interesting looking sunset photos. Winds stayed light. I also was able to gather some snow from about 100 feet down the south face to boil up a hot drink. The sun went down and I was treated to a half moon along with a lightning show far off in the southern sky from a dissipating thunderstorm.

**Meteorology  Chris:** I watched the satellite and radar closely during the week preceding Jon's trip into the Needle Mountains. It didn't look perfect. The first night of the trip I knew the afternoon thunderstorms would pass over and I told Jon to take advantage, even though he didn't receive some of my messages until he was safely off Eolus.

If you decide to tackle these peaks, start early and be efficient. These peaks form a high wall of granite. Dry, hot air from the deserts of New Mexico, Arizona, and Utah to the south and west ascend on the heels of the prevailing wind. This air slams into these peaks forcing the air to rise violently. Eolus Peak is the first peak the air runs into and almost always experiences storm development first. Some call Eolus a storm factory and I think this assessment is fair. Chicago Basin can be a dangerous place in the afternoon—full of lightning, hail, and downpours.

Sun setting on the Eolus Group.

# North Eolus Nap Time

**14,039 feet** (37° 37' 25" N; 107° 37' 14" W)

North Eolus, with Eolus to the southwest.

## The Eolus Batholith

Early in the morning from Eolus's summit and out my tent door you could look south and see the Durango Airport lights. You could see the lights of Bayfield and Ignacio, along with farms of the rural desert plateaus beyond. Before the sun came up you could see clear to New Mexico and Arizona and far west into Utah. From the highest point in the Needle Mountains you can see the entire collection of San Juan fourteeners, including Uncompaghre and Wetterhorn, where I was the week before. To the northwest are the Wilsons and El Diente, as well as Sneffels, my remaining summit bivys in the San Juans.

The entire complex of the Needle Mountains is part of the 1.7-billion-year-old Eolus Batholith. This batholith is well known for its high concentrations of quartz, feldspar, and pink granite combinations. Rectangular crystals of pink potassium feldspar and steeply inclined right-angled joints are responsible for the large angular blocks high on the peaks. The rosy feldspar is especially evident on the famous Catwalk connecting Eolus with its sub-summit to the north called North Eolus. North Eolus is not considered an official fourteener because the Catwalk connecting the two peaks only rises about 160 feet at its highest point, thus making North Eolus a bump on the ridge and yet named and above 14,000 feet.

# The Importance of Carrying a Good Map

I was finished crossing the Catwalk and encountered a guy who said he was from New York. He was coming off North Eolus after having mistaken it for Eolus. I see this all too many times. People always get the peaks wrong! That could lead them into trouble. Always carry maps and learn how to read them correctly while interpreting the terrain in the field! I could tell that the guy was inexperienced and unsure of himself. Sure, I was up there alone, but only after years of experience and knowledge of the peaks. He asked me how to get to the top of Eolus, but I explained to him that I didn't take the standard route past the Catwalk. Instead, I avoided the standard route on the southeast face that had treacherous snow and climbed directly up the northeast ridge on solid rock. He sat on the ridge and took a break. Meanwhile, I took my bivy sack and climbed up to North Eolus. In about ten minutes time I was on the summit. I took a short nap on North Eolus, and since it is one of the unofficial-official 14ers, took some excellent morning photos and then escaped down the snow chute below the southeast face. I still had two more nights in these mountains and bivys slated for Sunlight and Windom. It was about to get interesting.

Above: USGS benchmark on the summit.

Left: North Eolus (left) was reached by crossing the Catwalk from Eolus in the morning. Sunlight and Windom are seen along the eastern horizon (right).

# Sunlight Peak

## Summit Block Lightning

**14,059 feet** (37° 37' 38" N; 107° 35' 45" W)
**Bivy** July 8–9

**Meteorology   Chris:** I remember thinking, *This is going to be the worst night for Jon.* As expected, afternoon thunderstorms developed with some additional fuel from the monsoon. There was a two-hour break, allowing Jon to summit Sunlight, get the sunset photos, and then brace himself for a direct hit. These storms kept training over the Needle Range all night. It didn't look like the afternoon activity was going to die off at all. Radar at 10:00 p.m. showed a continuation of rain, lightning, and hail. I just prayed Jon found safe haven.

Twin Lakes in Upper Chicago Basin at 12,000 feet usually stay frozen until July in most years.

## Ten Peaks in and the Luck Finally Ran Out

On July 8, I "got into position" in my tent for the afternoon in-between Sunlight and Windom at 13,200 feet and waited out a massive thunder and hailstorm. This strategy of "getting into position" would become the standard on most peaks. I knew that a tent couldn't fit on Sunlight's summit, therefore setting up a safe haven with my tent to wait out weather was well worth it. I could simply use a bivy sack for the night on top. I ate dinner around 4:00 p.m. as the storms started to blow themselves out. From my intermediate camp at 13,200 feet, it wasn't going to take more than an hour to reach Sunlight's summit, even with overnight bivy gear. As the storms died out, I decided to start the climb at about 5:45 p.m. The route was an easy start, a contour on snow to Sunlight's southwest face and rubble gully at 13,500 feet, up to the connecting saddle between Sunlight and the Sunlight Spire at 13,750 feet, then a fun set of Class 3+ scrambling with a couple of Class 4 moves near the summit.

When I got to the last hundred feet or so of Sunlight, I could see a massive ring of thunderstorm clouds stretching in an arc from the southwest to the northwest. These thunderstorms stretched from the New Mexico/Colorado border to the La Plata Range, and then wrapped all the way north to the Wilson Massif, Telluride, Sneffels, and even over to Uncompaghre. The storm system was enormous, but careful review of the clouds and the prevailing flow of

Left: This rocky outcropping at 13,200 feet below Sunlight (left) and Sunlight Spire (right) served as an excellent base camp to wait out storms before dashing to the summit in an hour or less for both Sunlight and Windom on consecutive nights.

Above: Sunrise from Sunlight's summit after the electrical storm. Windom is seen in the distance to the south.

Top: While climbing to Sunlight's summit, the storm approached from the south of Sunlight Spire (left), and Windom (center).

Above: Storms were seen to the north of the summit block as well.

the upper level winds calmed my nerves for a moment. Fortunately, the storm movement was not in my immediate direction. When I reached the summit at about 7:00 p.m., I also noticed a large thunderstorm complex to the southeast and an even larger cumulonimbus cloud as far south as Farmington, nearly a hundred miles away in New Mexico. "Something to keep an eye out for in the next couple of hours," I said out loud.

## A Problematic Summit Block

I quickly set to work getting some summit shots and setting up my bivy sack. Sunlight Peak is famous in fourteener circles for its unique "summit block"— so unique and dangerous that most people don't actually climb to the true summit. There is a little concave flat spot just below the highest block, and that is where I set up my bivy sack for the night. The regular jointed rectangular granite is responsible for the patterns and orientation of these boulders near the summit.

With storms pretty much in every direction, I knew that I was in for a long night. I thought to myself, *There isn't a chance in hell I'm going to be spared this time.* As darkness fell, the lightning strikes became brighter and brighter, the thunder louder and louder. I watched the storms roll into the Needle Range from the south. My stomach was in knots, but I decided to ride out the storms. I wasn't going anywhere.

I remembered the "bolt-hole" and cavern directly below the summit block that I saw during my sunset photos. Well, it was time to "bolt" towards it now! It had to be safer than up on the top block. My pack was secure and covered up on a ledge (I would get it later) so I leapt out of my bivy sack, slipped my shoes on, picked up the entire bivy sack with my mat and sleeping bag, and ran for cover.

As I entered the small cavern, I felt another bolt of lightning and a crash of thunder almost instantaneously. Thinking I was going to be hit, I jumped into the cave, sprawled out my sack, and breathed a sigh of relief. At least I wasn't getting hit by the hail anymore. If the lightning was going to get me, it would have to come in and get me! There was barely enough room to lay down and a few rocks were underneath me, so I spent the next three hours listening to the hail, the rain, and of course an occasional lightning bolt. I barely slept, but the light show was spectacular.

# Windom Peak
### A Notch and a Rescue

**14,082 feet** (37° 37' 16" N; 107° 35' 31" W)
**Bivy** July 9–10

# Going for the Third Summit in a Row

I accomplished three peaks in two nights with two summit bivys—I was feeling pretty good. I heard my first rumble at about 1:30 p.m. as opposed to noon the day before. This was good news, in theory. After dinner at six o'clock, I started to climb the west ridge of Windom. From my "position camp" it was less than an hour to the top, and it only gets to Class 2+ at the most. I was excited that I had saved the easiest peak for last.

**Meteorology Chris:** In my gut I knew this group of peaks would be incredibly challenging weather-wise. Once you're committed to the Chicago Basin you feel the pressure to complete all the 14ers no matter the weather. I studied various satellite images before Jon departed. I concluded that afternoon thunderstorms fueled by a small surge of monsoon moisture appeared likely for nights two and three—the best moisture would arrive after night one. Thunderstorms during the monsoon season of July and August can last all night in some cases. Moisture can sit and linger over the Needle Range, so it might be a good idea to allow an extra day in case of bad weather. Jon somehow managed to find a way to get the bivys on those peaks done in succession, a feat that will be tough to duplicate.

## Witnessing a Rescue on Eolus

In a strange development, I watched a helicopter circle Eolus. I was looking directly west at the peak and the helicopter circled over the peak twice, then dropped down and landed on the point to the east and below the Catwalk, called Glacier Point (13,540 feet), which connects Eolus and North Eolus. The chopper landed for about ten minutes and I could see two figures on the ground. Maybe they were picking up someone who got injured? Then it flew down the south ridge toward lower Chicago Basin and then out of sight in the other direction heading due west. I later learned that two climbers fell from the snowfield on the southeast face of the peak. I snapped a few pictures. I wished it had been two nights earlier so I could've assisted with the rescue!

While we won't get into details of that day and the climbers that were injured on Eolus, the events were a sober reminder: the mountains make all the decisions. We can only control so much by being more efficient. Carry only essentials, especially an ice axe when traveling on snow, or avoid unstable snow altogether in the summer, especially near ledges. Be in excellent physical condition, move fast, know your route, your limitations, and make good decisions! I always respect the mountains and never let my guard down.

Large angular blocks guard Windom's summit.

## A Summit Notch Shelter

Meanwhile, I spent another slightly stormy but less terrifying night on the summit of Windom in my bivy sack in the notch you see here in the photo. The perfectly vertical and angular nature of the granite blocks on the summit of Windom are a textbook example of classic freeze-thaw mechanical weathering at its finest. The only regret I had was that I probably could have fit a tent near the top, but my bivy sack worked well in that notch.

Previous page: Sunrise.

Above: I spent another slightly stormy but less terrifying night on the summit of Windom in my bivy sack in the notch you see here.

# Mount Wilson
San Miguel Monarch

**14,246 feet** (37° 50' 21" N; 107° 59' 29" W)
**Bivy** July 13–14

**Meteorology  Chris:** I vividly remember Mount Wilson. Jon and I talked on the phone a couple of times while he was perched on Wilson's precarious summit. I felt good about Mount Wilson's weather forecast. A few dark clouds and that was it. I told Jon to hold firm on the summit.

Top: First light on Mount Wilson with El Diente in the distance.

Right: Monitoring the weather and writing observations from the top.

# Wilson Weather Window

I arrived on Mount Wilson's summit via Navajo Basin by 10:00 a.m. I finally had some good weather, although I was not letting my guard down after what happened on Sunlight Peak. By 4:00 p.m. I had managed to stay up there all day with the help of my knowledge of Colorado geography and flow of weather systems. For further confirmation, I had two phone conversations on the summit with Chris. He was manning his weather center in Denver, with both radar and satellite imagery pulled up. Chris was tracking some distant storms, but he wasn't worried and said to mainly expect a few dark cumulus clouds coming from the southwest. Fortunately we didn't have any thunderstorm development. I watched a few cells try to develop, but luckily they stayed away. This part of the project was like playing roulette. There were storms earlier that day around 2:00 p.m. to the west over by Moab, but they missed me. This kind of forecasting accuracy showed me I could at least come up here, set up my camp and have my bag and bivy sack ready to go with food and water. If a storm rolled in, I could quickly descend down into the valley, slide down the permanent snowfield, known as the Navajo Glacier, and return when conditions died down in time to shoot sunset photos and to stay the night. It was part skill, part luck.

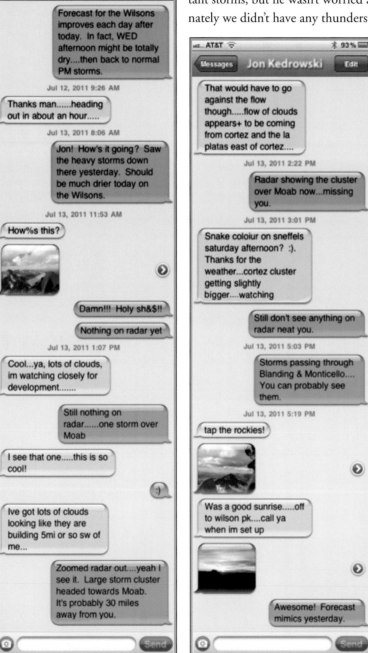

Left: Jon and Chris in constant communication monitoring the storms while Jon stayed on the summit of Mount Wilson all day on July 13.

Above: Sunrise on Mount Wilson with Wilson Peak to the left.

## Marmot Neighbors on a Narrow Perch

I had to move a few rocks to fit my tent up here, and somehow a few marmots came up to beg for food handouts. The summit of the peak is roughly fifteen feet by ten feet with lots of green and purple volcanic breccia and igneous intrusions. Some of the rock fragments off the northeast aspect are quite loose. El Diente sits to the west. The conditions were actually a bit icy on the granite and porphyry rocks. Snow was icy in the shade early that morning on my way to summiting this peak. I started at roughly 7:00 a.m. from Navajo Lake and was on the summit by 10:00 a.m., even with a heavy pack and treacherous conditions. This is one of Colorado's toughest fourteeners, and one of only six Class 4 peaks that have to be climbed and camped on. Carrying a heavier pack can be tough and increases fatigue. I was careful getting down the final section in the morning, which is a Class 4 face, with a few interesting moves. I actually chose to down-climb the northern spine of the peak just below the summit. The rock is safer, although low Class 5, and I know every step blindfolded!

Left: All packed up and ready to depart the summit of Mount Wilson.

Above: North faces of Gladstone (left), Mount Wilson (center), and El Diente (right), from an old mining claim at 13,000 feet in Upper Navajo Basin.

# Wilson Peak

Tap the Rockies

**14,017 feet** (37° 51' 37" N; 107° 59' 05" W)
**Bivy** July 14–15

Top: Northeast view from the summit. Views from Telluride in the valley (right) clear to Grand Mesa on the horizon (left).

Right: Sunrise with (left to right) Glastone Peak, Mount Wilson, and El Diente dominating the backdrop.

## A Well Known Icon

I tapped the Rockies, literally! Wilson Peak is the Coors can icon. There are people all over the world that hold this mountain in their hands and do twelve-ounce curls on a daily basis. The sun was out and things looked favorable as I arrived on the summit after traversing over from Mount Wilson. The day was considerably drier than yesterday, and the views were even more stunning than before. It was so clear from the Grand Mesa to the north, out into Utah to the west, south to Durango and Cortez, with just some small cumulus over the San Juans to the east and southeast.

## Mount Wilson Stock

Silver was found here in the 1870s by prospectors in Silver Pick Basin, just to the north of Wilson Peak. A.D. Wilson and Franklin Rhoda were among the first to climb both Wilson Peak and Mount Wilson as part of the Hayden Surveys in September 1874. The Wilson Stock consists primarily of dark grey massive plutonic rocks, 26 million years in the making. Fine-grained white and grey granite dominates the summit, and the expansive 150-yard summit ridge is guarded on all sides by steep down-sloping drop-offs. Telluride conglomerate and purple volcanic breccia can also be found in the broken cliffs throughout the entire massif.

Wilson Peak's standard route does not exceed Class 3, but there are a multitude of ledges and sharp and rotten rock toward the summit that you have to overcome. I recall making it up to this summit for the first time in a pouring rainstorm in 1999. The last 250 feet were pretty deadly. This trip by comparison was pretty benign on the summit pitch, even with overnight gear and a tent. But yes, camping on these peaks is a whole new challenge, and so far I am holding my own. Fortunately, the weather was exceptional. The winds were light and the nights were crisp from the time I ascended Mount Wilson until the morning I descended Wilson Peak two days later.

Top: Sunset looking east, full moon rising.

Above: Wilson Peak seen from the south from the slopes of Mount Wilson.

# El Diente Peak The Tooth

**14,159 feet** (37° 50' 23" N; 108° 00' 19" W)
**Bivy** July 15–16

## Sub-summit of Mount Wilson

El Diente means "the tooth," and this description is very appropriate. El Diente rises like a prominent incisor about a mile and a half to the west of Mount Wilson. At 14,159 feet, but only 259 feet above the connecting saddle from Mount Wilson, it could be considered just a bump on the ridge and not even a fourteener at all. Even though it's classified as unofficial, I would call it official because it is named on USGS maps and is a very formidable climb. Because of the unrelenting vertical gain and sustained difficulty, I would probably place El Diente in the top five in regards to difficulty out of all the Colorado 14ers. On this particular adventure, El Diente proved itself worthy of the top five. It is hard enough to climb the peak with only a day pack, but to add the weight of overnight bivy gear and the snowy conditions makes it even more rigorous.

Opposite: Abundant wildflowers above Navajo Lake, located at the base of El Diente.

Above left: Looking east at sunset toward Wilson Peak (center) and Mount Wilson (right). Staying on El Diente completed all three peaks in three consecutive nights.

Above right: No room for a tent as the sun sets.

## Farthest from Denver and Isolated in the San Miguels

Given the difficulty and accessibility of El Diente, it is no wonder that in all five of my ascents of the peak that I have never seen another person on the peak above the valley floor. Tucked away in the sub-range of the San Juans known as the San Miguel Mountains, El Diente is almost 300 miles as the crow flies from Denver. It's a long drive for most folks, which means the majority of climbers don't spend time there.

In 2008 Chris joined me for a fall ascent, and on that trip I remembered specifically that there was no room for a tent on that summit. Chris remembers that particular ascent: "We climbed the north face after a foot of new snow. Even to this day, that was one of the most physically draining 14er ascents I can remember. It was almost like going to the dentist—"the tooth" took a bite out of us that day."

On this trip, I ventured to the south side of El Diente via Kilpacker Basin, an isolated and remote basin with waterfalls and only a primitive trail. To build a modern trail into this basin would be devastating in such a pristine setting of wildflowers and giant elk. Most climbers currently access El Diente by the much easier Navajo Basin approach, and it should be kept that way. I carried only an overnight bivy sack and found a couple of nice protective nooks to set up for the evening on the summit. I enjoyed a lack of wind for the third consecutive night and slept out directly on the dark plutonic granite summit block. Massive grey granite also dominates this peak, especially along the summit ridge and along the 2,500-foot high north face, which I chose to descend after a restful night on top of one of Colorado's most precarious summits. This marked three consecutive nights on the peaks of the Wilson Massif—something that has probably never been done before. I only had Sneffels left in order to likely become the first to spend the night on every fourteener summit in the San Juans.

**Meteorology  Chris:** No matter how you slice it, El Diente Peak is an arduous climb. It's not something you want to repeat because of bad weather. Jon and I talked on the phone a few times about the best day to attempt El Diente, near the tailend of his stint on the Wilson Massif. Once Jon was set up that afternoon on El Diente, we talked again a couple times on the phone. I didn't see anything on radar that worried me. The weather window I had forecast was materializing. A few dark clouds circled El Diente but nothing developed. Jon was in the clear.

# Mount Sneffels

## Circumnavigation

**14,150 feet** (38° 00' 14" N; 107° 47' 32" W)
**Bivy** July 16–17

**Meteorology  Chris:** The July monsoon was really kicking in when we tackled Sneffels. I distinctly remember watching the radar and satellite closely the day before I was meeting Jon in Ridgway. A moderate surge of monsoon moisture was moving north out of Arizona flowing through Durango. My analysis ended up being correct. We hiked the first part of the long circuit up Blaine Basin just dodging a few rain showers—no lightning. Skies cleared that night. We awoke to rain showers and dark clouds moving in from the south, signaling that it was time to descend as the sun came up over the eastern horizon.

Mt. Sneffels experiences two important weather features: 1) Typical daily afternoon thunderstorms, and 2) Leftover monsoon precipitation that typically hits the southern San Juans first then sweeps north toward the Sneffels Massif, leaving the southern Grand Valley in a rain shadow.

Left: A grand view looking south to the Wilson Massif (left horizon) at sunset.

Above: Sunset on Sneffels, too rocky for a tent.

Left: Chris following Jon up the final section of the south couloir en route to the summit.

## Teamwork Makes Sneffels Possible

Going for four peak bivys in four consecutive nights, and my eighth summit bivy in ten days, I was running on fumes. Coming off of El Diente Peak that morning, I received a text from Chris saying that he'd be driving all the way from Denver on that Friday to meet me in Ridgway that afternoon. Chris wanted to join the party. I was excited to celebrate the completion of the entire San Juans with Chris.

I was the one climbing and camping on all of these summits, but Chris provided a huge psychological, mental, and meteorological boost to this endeavor. When Chris joined me for the summit bivy on Sneffels, his physical presence made all the difference in this Herculean effort to finish off the San Juans. Chris's assessments of storms were invaluable, and even though I, too, could see the storms, his accurate pinpoint forecasts gave me peace of mind to know that I wasn't going to get hit by the storms.

## A Monarch with No Place for a Tent

The thunderstorms that day tracked from Durango, over the Needles, across Sneffels, and then directly into the Grand Valley and Grand Mesa. Except for a few sprinkles, we stayed mainly dry. The wildflowers at tree line were stunning. Once above the basin, the long eastern flank of Sneffels rises gradually, and even in July was very snow loaded, but made for an excellent snow climb and true mountaineering experience. I could tell Chris was really enjoying this route up Sneffels. The seldom-climbed north side routes have a few snow couloirs of 40–60 degrees, but nothing that couldn't be climbed without crampons in the warm overcast afternoon. Many of these classic couloirs are cut along veins and faults, which have left the gabbro and dark granitic rocks highly fractured and broken. This explains why it was difficult to put a tent on the summit, as the volcanic breccia, conglomerate, and jagged granite textures guarded the vicinity of the summit. We each opted for an open bivy, using the abundance of unstable rocks to build some small windbreaks to stop the 30 mph gusts coming up from the south. In the morning, to beat the oncoming storm, we opted to circle Mount Sneffels clockwise, following the spectacular Highline–Blue Lakes circuit.

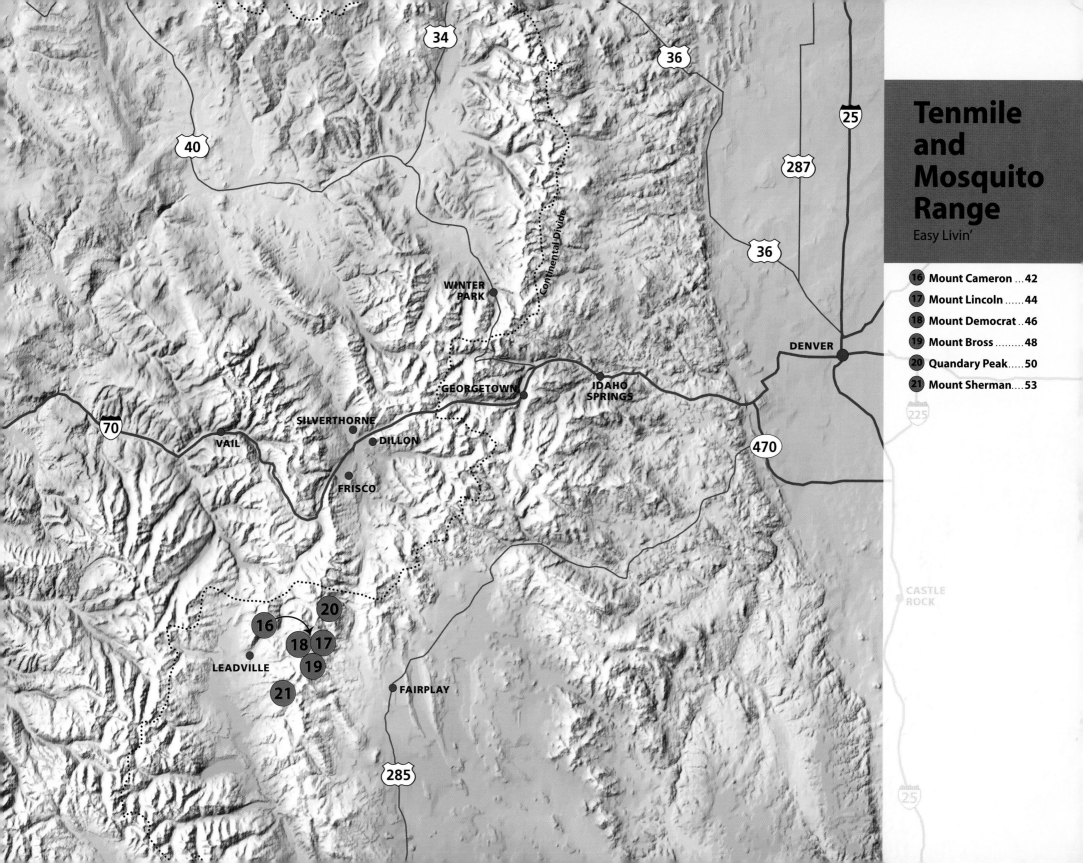

# Tenmile and Mosquito Range

*Easy Livin'*

# Mount
# Cameron Official Unofficial

**14,238 feet** (39° 21' 02" N; 106° 06' 43" W) • **Afternoon Nap** July 19

Opposite: Cameron's summit, with Lincoln less than a mile away.

## The Start of a New Mountain Range

I was well rested after a visit to my Mom and Dad's house in Vail for a couple of days following the completion of the San Juans. I proceeded with the project and drove over to the Kite Lake trailhead on Tuesday afternoon to work on four fourteeners: Cameron, Lincoln, Democrat, and Bross. The weather for the past few days was typical for this time of year—really awful in the afternoon with strong electrical thunderstorms and lots of monsoon rain. Not the best weather for hitting a peak in the afternoon. What was really challenging about this project was that I was breaking a lot of rules regarding peak climbing in Colorado in the summertime. The most important rule is to stay off high ridges and peaks after lunchtime!

I arrived at the Kite Lake trailhead around 5:00 p.m., and to my delight there was blue sky and many of the afternoon storms seemed to have moved out. This set of peaks, as long as the weather cooperated, would be pretty easy compared to the long days and technical climbs in the San Juans. The Kite Lake trailhead is at 12,000 feet, leaving only a little over 2,000 vertical feet on a well-worn trail for each of the peaks in this group. My strategy was to basically car camp from the lake, meaning to hang out at a lower elevation each day, and each summit was no more than an hour to an hour and a half to the top even with my overnight gear. Each morning I could wake up on the summits, get the photos, and pack up, returning to the safety of my vehicle for a day of eating, writing, and taking naps!

## Sub-Summit of Lincoln

I quickly tossed my overnight gear together, including sleeping bag, bivy sack, and tent, along with food and water, and I started up toward the saddle between Democrat and Lincoln a little after 5:30 p.m. At about 6:15 p.m. I was up to 13,400 feet and on the ridge making my way east toward Lincoln and Cameron.

At 6:45 p.m. I was walking across another official-unofficial fourteener—Mount Cameron. Cameron is really only a connecting highpoint on the ridge between Lincoln and Democrat and also Lincoln and Bross. It looks like a pile of rubble from the days of silver mining in this area, many of the rocks consisting of Paleozoic sandstone, shale, and tinted limestone. It is a named summit, but since it only rises 157 feet from Lincoln and even less from the other peaks, it does not count as an official fourteener. Just for fun, I set up my bivy sack for a nap once again. Maybe someday I will spend a full night up on that little insignificant summit, but for that evening it was off to get set up on Lincoln, as skies continued to clear.

Cameron's gentle east ridge.

# Mount Lincoln

## Highest in the Tenmile/Mosquito

**14,286 feet** 39° 21' 05" N; 106° 06' 42" W)
**Bivy** July 19–20

**Meteorology Chris:** Afternoon thunderstorms developed each day directly on top of the Lincoln Group. Fog developed as well. It was a nasty mix of conditions. Jon dialed-in and made incredibly fast ascents to set up gear each evening before sunset. I was monitoring conditions over the Lincoln Group in real-time on radar. If I saw anything specific, I would update Jon with text messages.

Right: Morning fog lingers prior to sunrise on Lincoln.

## Dodging Storms

From the summit of Cameron, I had my cell phone turned on. From that vantage point I could see some storms down to the south over either Salida or the Sangre de Cristos; a large storm system to the west toward Eagle, Gypsum, and Glenwood Springs; and a giant storm cell stretching out to the east from Pikes Peak and Colorado Springs all the way north to Boulder and even up toward Longs Peak. Once again I had Chris alert me that the two largest systems, to the west and east of me, both had zero chance of coming toward me. I could see this from the clouds and their movements as well. What concerned me was the cell to the south. Monsoon flows usually come from that direction. Fortunately, Chris kept tabs on it and also noted that the storm's strength was dying out with the setting sun and that it probably wouldn't make it past Buena Vista to the south. I continued on to Lincoln's summit.

## Summit Sill

At 7:15 p.m. I reached the summit. Lincoln looks like some sort of volcanic neck or sill, although the majority of the rock on the summit appears to be granite and porphyry that has taken much more time to weather away compared to the surrounding sedimentary layers of rock. It juts out like a nipple of some sort, making it actually a relatively small summit, and it's the eighth highest peak in Colorado. In a fortunate turn of events, not only was the weather holding, but right on the summit within feet of the highest point there was a great place for a tent that was absent of sharp rocks—a nice flat area of dirt about the size of my tent. I knew I'd be comfortable that night, especially since I brought a luxury item up from the car with me, something I never ever carry—a soft feather pillow! Perhaps somebody else had bivyed up there before, more than likely. The winds picked up after sunset, so I gathered up some rocks to anchor my tent.

In the morning I awoke to a brilliant cloudy sunrise and strong winds. After quickly taking down my tent, I rapidly descended back to Kite Lake for a large breakfast.

A well-worn trail leads to the final summit pinnacle, with storms staying far to the east.

# Mount Democrat

## Molybdenum Summit

**14,148 feet** (39° 20' 23" N; 106° 08' 24" W)
**Bivy** July 20–21

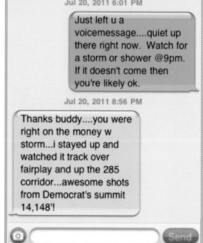

Jul 20, 2011 6:01 PM

Just left u a voicemessage....quiet up there right now. Watch for a storm or shower @9pm. If it doesn't come then you're likely ok.

Jul 20, 2011 8:56 PM

Thanks buddy....you were right on the money w storm...i stayed up and watched it track over fairplay and up the 285 corridor...awesome shots from Democrat's summit 14,148'!

Top: Scattered clouds from diminishing storms make for brilliant sunsets.

Above: Democrat's summit with Lincoln, Cameron, and Bross in the distance.

Early morning light and hundred-mile views.

## Accurate Forecasting Pays Off

The afternoon was clear and I ate dinner around 4:30 p.m. Wednesday. I left the comforts of Kite Lake and my truck to head up the southeast face and ridge of Democrat at about 5:30 p.m., basically a trail to the summit, nothing too special, but great views.

When I reached the summit around 7:00 p.m., I got a weather update from Chris. He said to keep an eye on the southern sky—maybe a storm by 9:00 p.m. But it was clear at 7:00 p.m., with a few clouds down near the Sangre de Cristos, so I set to work putting up my tent, and had it up in light winds and sunshine around 7:30. I could see the recently re-opened Climax Mine to the west and also the highest two mountains in Colorado to the southwest: Elbert and Massive. I could see clear to the Maroon Bells, Snowmass, and Capitol in the Elk Range in the far west. Sure enough, by 9:00 p.m., a storm rumbled to the southeast over Fairplay and South Park, but it didn't come up the mountain—it stayed away but provided a dramatic backdrop for evening photos.

## Climax Mine

Molybdenum is a metal alloy that is added to iron in the steel-making process. This alloy helps strengthen steel for major industrial, building, and equipment production uses. The majority of the molybdenum is taken from the vicinity of Fremont Pass and the Climax Mine that resumed production in 2011, a few miles west of Democrat off of CO Highway 91. Some of the richest concentrations are found within the granite basement rocks of the Mosquito Fault, a north-south trending zone that is visible from the summit of Democrat to the west. I pitched my tent within feet of the true summit, and built a small summit wall for wind protection, taking advantage of the 1.4- to 1.7-billion-year-old coarse-grained streaky granite that surely has reasonable concentrations of molybdenum minerals. However, it was the first summit in a few that had no wind all night long and it was relatively warm, too. I fell asleep fast and slept all night!

**Meteorology** Chris: Tackling the four fourteeners of the Lincoln Group in one day requires a solid weather window. Jon would sleep on the summit of each on separate nights, so my job was to identify a good weather window for him to dash to the summit each evening. I never did find the perfect window, but this is one of the lessons of this project. In less than optimal conditions you follow your gut and devise a strategy. Fast, efficient hikers can often work around bad weather. This is exactly what Jon did.

# Mount Bross

## Prospector's Paradise

**14,172 feet** (39° 20' 07" N; 106° 06' 27" W)
**Bivy** July 21–22

Right: Sunset among the rain shafts.

Sunrise.

# Bross, AKA "South Cameron"

For the third consecutive summit bivy in a row, I departed after an afternoon dinner and this time it was to Bross. In an hour flat I was on the summit in clearing skies. The connecting saddle between Lincoln and Bross holds barely a 300-foot rise, and therefore Bross is sometimes not considered an official fourteener. Because of this, Bross is sometimes called South Cameron by the locals. Bross is probably Colorado's flattest and largest summit. You could fit more than three football fields and four large houses up on that summit area! In typical fashion, I set up my tent, and this time the winds were high for most of the evening and night. Fortunately, there was a large rock shelter at the true summit, so I set up the tent there for photos.

## Mining Claims

Some of the mining claims from the 1800s are still owned and often prospected even today. Silver has historically been the most popular ore taken from these broad hillsides. Four-wheel-drive vehicles can actually drive to the summit of Bross on one of the many mining trails on the east aspect of the peak. Post-laramide porphyry is the most prevalent rock near the summit. A mine on the southeast end of the large summit area has been known to produce the brilliant red mineral known as rhodochrosite (manganese carbonate, $MnCO_3$), the Colorado state mineral.

Since I knew it was going to be a clear night, I left my tent up but slept out under the stars, which were spectacular. After sunset, I fell asleep and only woke a few times all night with temps in the mid-twenties!

# Quandary Peak Easy Evening

**14,265 feet** (39° 23' 50" N; 106° 06' 23" W)
**Bivy** July 22–23

Opposite: Jon and Chris celebrate the 20th bivy of the project on a very warm evening.

Right: Jon building a wall to block light prevailing westerlies while sleeping outside.

**Meteorology  Chris:** I saw a large weather window for Quandary Peak. The monsoon plume drifted east for about three days, which allowed for unparalleled views during sunset and sunrise. Always consider the wind while climbing peaks in the Tenmile Range—only during the summer do winds calm down. Most of the time, winter wind speeds normally exceed 30 mph sustained. During monsoon season the daily build-up of thunderstorms begin along the Tenmile Range, reach maturity, then travel east across the Continental Divide, typically impacting thunderstorm activity across the Front Range peaks.

## The Quandary: Sleeping in the Tent or Outside?

Just like the previous week on Sneffels, Chris met me in Breckenridge to join me for my fourth summit in four nights. I was pretty tired from a series of summit bivys on the Tenmile peaks that week, and his presence gave me a huge lift once again.

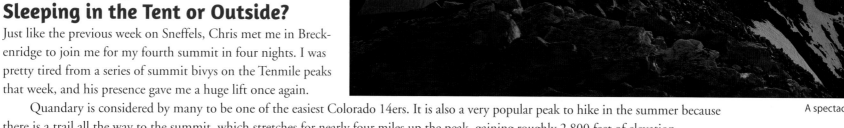

A spectacular sunset.

Quandary is considered by many to be one of the easiest Colorado 14ers. It is also a very popular peak to hike in the summer because there is a trail all the way to the summit, which stretches for nearly four miles up the peak, gaining roughly 2,800 feet of elevation.

Chris and I convened for a "pre-game" meal of sorts. We ate at a popular Mexican restaurant, stuffing ourselves for the climb ahead, and made our way to the Quandary trailhead, just south of Breckenridge off of Colorado Highway 9.

Sunrise alpenglow with views clear to the Elk Mountains.

## Metamorphic Anticline Basement

Our plan was to carry just overnight gear, and enough food and water for the evening and a small breakfast. No stoves, and no unnecessary gear. This classic "dash and crash" strategy was becoming common for this project. Go as fast and as light as possible, and in this case it was—climbing to the summit in only ninety minutes. When you know there is going to be good weather you can get away with this strategy, but always climb and camp on peaks within your limits, prepared for all conditions. Quandary would be an excellent fourteener as a first try at an overnight bivy—the trail is relatively straightforward, and the summit has lots of space.

On that night, our biggest dilemma was deciding whether or not to use a tent. Quandary's long summit ridge has plenty of room for a tent, yet metamorphic biotite gneiss and migmatite with various dikes of pegmatite, granite, and porphyry make the top fairly rugged. There are plenty of excellent metamorphic and igneous rock veins in which to select large blocks to build wind walls, although on that flawless night the wind was the least of our worries. I'd say the mountain goats and our residual stomach cramps from the afternoon's pre-trip meal were more of a nuisance that day!

# Mount Sherman

## Simple Silver

**14,036 feet** (39° 13' 30" N; 106° 10' 11" W)
**Bivy** July 24–25

**Meteorology  Chris:** Sherman didn't warrant any special weather concerns. I knew Jon could ascend and descend Sherman quickly in case of a rogue thunderstorm, and in this case I wasn't expecting any significant weather. There were storms to the east of Jon that night, and moving away from him, so I kept tabs on the radar until the storms fell apart after sunset.

Evening on a windy summit with some curious visitors.

Sunrise on Sherman and the vast expanse of South Park to the east.

Columbines accenting the hike up Iowa Gulch.

## Tenmile/Mosquito Finale

At five in the afternoon, I took a leisurely stroll up the southwest ridge and slopes of Sherman from Iowa Gulch for an hour and a half to reach Sherman's long summit by 6:30 p.m. I was greeted by mountain goats and an American flag, and put my tent just below the top on a nice platform shielded by some rocks. The wind was very strong from the west all night long. Climbing a relatively easy beginner-style fourteener like Sherman was a great way to complete my second mountain range of the six major Colorado mountain ranges. Sherman would be a spectacular fourteener summit bivy for anyone trying to camp on a summit for the first time.

## Silver Riches and Mineral Prizes

Slopes on the southeast and southwestern flanks of Sherman were mined until 1982, yielding over $100 million in silver. The porphyritic igneous rocks that make up the entire peak are part of an igneous sill that was formed in the Laramide Orogeny. Metals in addition to silver include zinc and lead mineralized crystals, often found in the underground cavern systems naturally formed in the lower layers of dolostones and from human-created mine shafts.

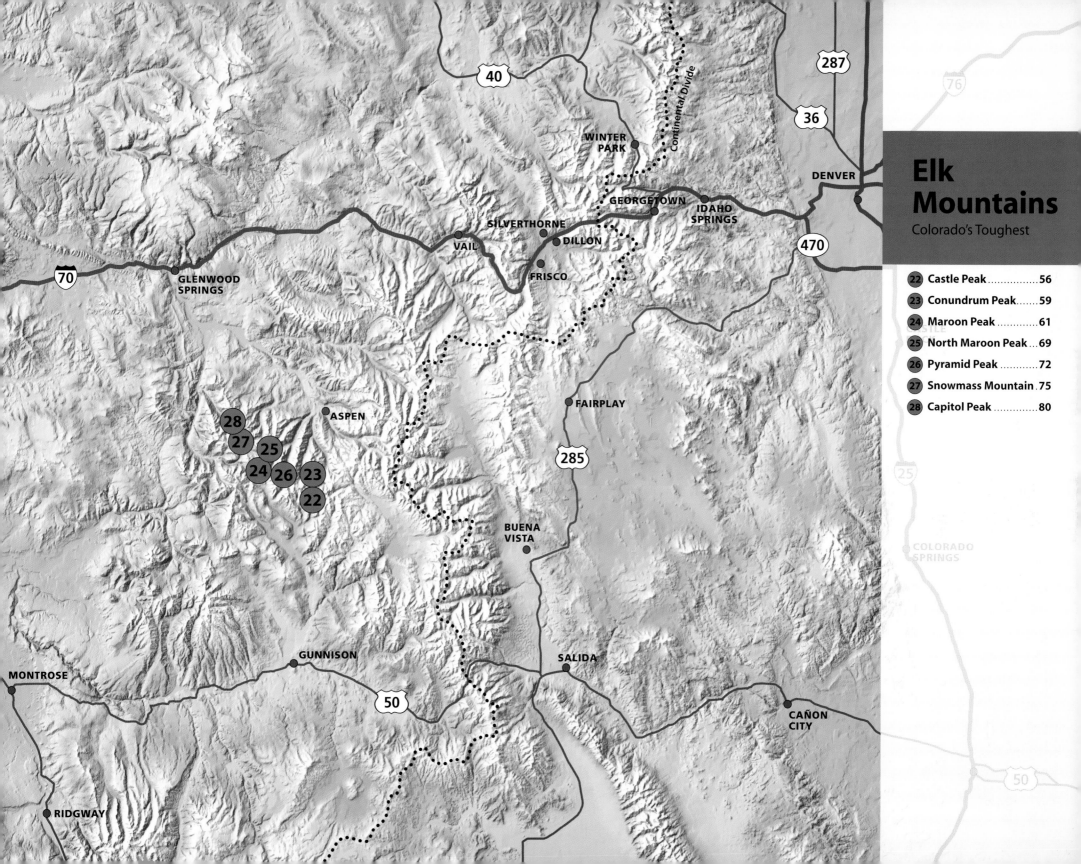

# Elk
# Mountains
Colorado's Toughest

# Castle
# Peak Elk Range
High Point

**14,265 feet** (39° 00' 35" N; 106° 51' 41" W)
**Bivy** July 25–26

## Summer Monsoon in Full Force

In terms of scenery I couldn't see much last night, just lots of water on the way up the trail and waterfalls from snowmelt. I had waited in my truck for a nasty electrical storm to pass in Lower Montezuma Basin at about 10,400 feet from 4:00 to 6:00 p.m.

In the previous five or six times that I climbed Castle from this route (I've also climbed some other routes up there), I have been able to drop down and go from the first creek crossing at 10,300 feet to the summit with a day pack in about two and a half hours. So once the weather cleared, I put on my overnight gear, and went as light as I could for the summit.

It stayed overcast all evening. At 7:00 p.m. I was to the end of the road at 13,000 feet in Upper Montezuma Basin. This year there was lots of snow in the upper basin and a couple of snow chutes to climb, which I absolutely love! Castle can sometimes make you feel like you're deep in the Alps or even in the Andes.

I made quick work of the first set of chutes and then had to really put the hammer down to gain the northwest ridge via a 50-degree chute sans crampons and only an ice axe.

Once on the ridge I saw a "wall of water" storm coming from the southwest, and knew I had to get to the summit fast in order to put up my tent before the storm.

**Meteorology Chris:** It was the start of the Elk Mountains. Jon was dancing on thin ice when he attempted Castle Peak. A clear-cut monsoon surge was slamming into the Elks. It was an important milestone of this project. Sometimes you have to operate in bad weather if and only if you are 100 percent certain of what's occurring in the atmosphere. I watched radar very closely as Jon ascended Castle Peak. I didn't see any lightning with the evening thunderstorms—it looked primarily like slow air ascent and cooler air dominating the process. This analysis matched with what Jon was seeing on the ground—we texted back and forth. Fog developed that night and completely shrouded the Elks. Evening fog can indicate that the atmosphere is just not primed for lightning. Jon hunkered down in his tent and slept through a night with zero visibility.

Opposite: A calm misty morning.

Above: Small rock shelter on the summit.

Below: Castle's narrow northwest ridge and the towers of Maroon Formation granite.

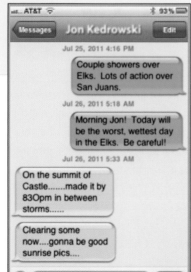

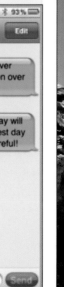

Jon Kedrowski

Jul 25, 2011 4:16 PM

Couple showers over Elks. Lots of action over San Juans.

Jul 26, 2011 5:18 AM

Morning Jon! Today will be the worst, wettest day in the Elks. Be careful!

Jul 26, 2011 5:33 AM

On the summit of Castle.......made it by 830pm in between storms......

Clearing some now....gonna be good sunrise pics....

Right: Waterfalls converging from Montezuma Basin (right), and Pearl Pass (left).

Below: Castle in good weather on a clear summer evening in 2009.

## Small Summit and Castle Creek Fault Zone

I made the summit at about 8:30 p.m., and got the tent up in the nick of time on the flat triangular summit. Lightning wasn't in this storm, just heavy rain for a couple of hours, but I was nice and dry and there wasn't much wind. Castle Peak, the highest peak in the Elk Mountains, is just southeast of the Castle Creek Fault Zone, which is responsible for the natural hot springs in the lower valleys nearby. Flat beds of the Maroon Formation give the peak its metamorphic rock character, and keep the summit nice and flat for an excellent bivy site. Extensive bodies of nearly 40-million-year-old granite are the basis of the peak with sandstone converted to grey quartzite, shale to greenish-grey hornfels, and limestone to grey and greenish marble. All these combinations are quite unique and different than the additional peaks in the remainder of the Elk range to the north.

In the morning I woke at 5:00 a.m., got a few morning photos, but there was lots of fog and rain was intermittent again. The forecast called for cloudy skies and socked-in rain all day, so I departed the summit quickly and headed over to Conundrum Peak to take a nap.

# Conundrum Peak Napping Dilemma

**14,060 feet** (39° 00' 56" N; 106° 51' 39" W)
**Morning Nap** July 26

Above and below: Monsoon moisture was threatening to engulf Conundrum's twin summit all morning long.

Right: The storm approaches Conundrum.

Below: Conundrum Hot Springs.

## Puzzled by Hot Springs Long Ago

From 6:00 to 7:30 a.m. I climbed down and over to Conundrum at 14,060 feet. I took a nap and shot a few nap bivy photos since Conundrum is not an official fourteener, but it is named.

Fog lifted momentarily to give glimpses of the remainder of the Elk Mountains. Down in the valley to the northwest, the Conundrum Hot Springs came into view for only a few moments. Early prospectors in the 1800s were literally in a conundrum over why and how these hot springs could exist so high and isolated in this lonesome corner of the Elk Mountains. Because the Castle Creek Fault Zone passes just to the northwest of the peaks, the valley in the vicinity of the hot springs provides a way for magma below the ground to push up into water that is found just below the surface. The boiling water cools to a comfortable 100°F near the surface and creates the highest natural hot springs in North America, at 11,200 feet. With thick fog and monsoonal rain bearing down on me that morning, I certainly longed for a hot dip in those springs!

Just before 8:00 a.m. I departed the soggy summit and went back to the chute leading east off of the northwest ridge. I dropped off the upper ridge of magnetite and made a quick exit boot skiing down the sweet snow chute to the safety of the talus and rock glaciers in the valley below. I would wait for a spell of better weather to allow me to tackle the Maroon Bells and Pyramid next, in three consecutive nights.

# Maroon Peak Foggy Icon

**14,156 feet** (39° 04' 15" N; 106° 59' 20" W)
**Bivy** July 27–28

**Meteorology  Chris:** During our ascent we watched large thunderstorms develop and track from south to east. I kept a close eye on radar and I liked what I was seeing. I had anticipated this kind of storm track and it was playing out perfectly. We could see frequent lightning and rain shafts hanging over the Sawatch Range to the east.

During the night heavy fog developed in the surrounding valleys below 12,000 feet. I woke up several times and watched the fog ebb and flow—for a meteorologist this is quite exhilarating. The fog thickened and eventually rose to over 14,000 feet, shrouding all of the Elk Mountain peaks. Why? Two days of heavy rain preceeded our arrival. Combine rain with a moist monsoonal flow and the recipe was perfect for night-time radiational fog. The Elks are known for their rugged geometry. Mountain range geometry plays a direct role in thunderstorm formation. The more jagged the mountain range, the more violent the afternoon storms.

Right: Maroon Bells from Maroon Lake.

Left: Carefully navigating Cartoon Ridge.

Right: Sunset.

Bottom right: Sunrise.

### The Magnificent yet Deadly Bells via "Cartoon Ridge"

Maroon Peak was the objective, via the south ridge. I call this "Cartoon Ridge" because when you see the peak from Maroon Lake, you climb up the face to gain the ridge on the left skyline of Maroon Peak. The last 1,000 feet you circle to the back of the peak on a series of ledges and faces that wind all the way around, like you are in one of those cartoons trying to get to the top of a mountain.

To get on the ridge, you have to master the south face first. This face rises from the valley nearly 2,500 feet in less than a mile to gain the ridge at 13,000 feet.

The south face took a long time, and the ledges were pretty fun as well. Considering Chris and I had heavy packs, we were thrilled with our time to the top, taking about three hours and forty-five minutes from Maroon Lake.

## Sedimentary Shale Summit

We quickly set up camp and monitored the weather closely. I found a sweet spot to put the tent, right on the summit block of the ridge crest. All the storms died off so we went to bed after the sun set. Red sandstone, shale, and even conglomerate rock dominate the composition of the Maroon Bells. The red color of these rocks gives the Maroon Bells their name, the color deriving from oxidation of iron minerals exposed to air under desert conditions from ancient evaporating seabeds millions of years ago before they were uplifted to their present position. Sediment was laid down, compacted, and hardened into layers, or "strata," which give the peak its distinct bell-shaped appearance from most vantage points.

# Traverse of the Bells

**Maroon Peak** 14,156 feet; 9:00 a.m.
**Saddle of Bell Chord Col** 13,780 feet; 9:30 a.m.
**North Maroon Peak** 14,014 feet; 10:00 a.m.
**Traverse** July 28

*Efficiency from peak to peak lowers your risk in the danger zone.*

**Meteorology Chris:** The Maroon Bell Traverse is challenging in dry weather, so any deviation in weather conditions is important to note before committing. We woke up to freezing fog and near-zero visibility. We had completed the traverse together on prior occasions, so we knew each step from memory. In fact, we've done the traverse before in complete snow conditions.

Once the fog broke around 9:00 a.m. I knew the weather would hold all day. Anyone interested in attempting the traverse needs to doublecheck the weather forecast and constantly diagnose it while in the field. Sometimes a foggy morning can indicate extra available moisture to fuel afternoon thunderstorms.

## Red, Rugged, and Rotten

On the Maroon Bells, loose and rotten rock is obvious, transformed by thousands or even millions of years of freeze-and-thaw mechanical weathering. The slabs of shale and brittle pieces of rock accumulate along every step of a climber's route to the summit. The twenty- to forty-foot thickness and unique northerly orientation of the ledges—roughly fifteen degrees from horizontal upon the sedimentary strata—give the Bells their famous silhouette, while also contributing to the "cartoon-like" appearance. The geologic geometry makes route finding an adventure during every ascent.

Awe-inspiring views of the entire Elk Range while climbing the Maroon Bells are a constant reminder that you are in Colorado's finest mountain range.

Chris carefully crossing a narrow ledge.

Maroon Peak.

5th class summit pitch leading to North Maroon.

Southeast ridge crest.

North Maroon Peak.

The halfway point—peering down the Bell Chord Couloir.

Above: Chris on a snowy Maroon Bells traverse in 2010.

Top: North Maroon Peak.

# North Maroon Peak Poker in the Sky

**14,014 feet** (39° 04' 23" N; 106° 59' 18" W)
**Bivy** July 28–29

Sunset colors over Pyramid (left), and Maroon (right).

Sunset.

Sunrise: Snowmass and Capitol seen to the north (right).

## Texas Hold 'Em at 14,000 feet

It was a nice series of ledges and fun up-climbs to get to North Maroon's summit before 10:30 a.m. It took less than an hour and a half from South Maroon, and we took our time. North Maroon is not an official fourteener by the 300-foot rule, yet the peak is so iconic and difficult that nobody questions its status and it is therefore considered an official fourteener.

The day's fog was burning off, so I spent about two hours building a nice rock shelter and tent platform directly on the summit. Chris went to work getting water for us by collecting water in our bottles from dripping snowmelt from a chunk of snow just feet from the summit.

We spent the rest of the afternoon watching for storms. We played cards and likely enjoyed the highest hand of Texas Hold 'Em ever to be played in the state of Colorado!

**Meteorology  Chris:** After the freezing fog on Maroon Peak dissolved, we were left with an incredibly calm day on North Maroon. I could tell by the prevailing wind that most of the afternoon storm activity was being pushed east of the Elk Mountains. There was nothing to the south or west—we were in the clear.

North Maroon can be a dangerous place during bad weather—it's a Class 4 descent. Don't get caught on its summit during the afternoon unless you're 100 percent sure what the weather is going to do.

## An Ancient Seabed Bivy

The compact sedimentary rock at this elevation wasn't always this high in the sky. Sandstone and shale caprock on the summit of North Maroon was formed at an ocean bottom known as the "Central Colorado Trough" 250 million years ago, prior to the Laramide Orogeny. You can see the resemblance of an ocean bottom on rocks right next to my bivy site directly on the summit. These petrified ocean bottoms have distinct ripples and were raised to the mountaintops when the Rocky Mountains were uplifted long ago. I literally had my head in the sand that night on the summit while I slept soundly.

Sunset over the Maroon Bells (center), from Pyramid Peak's summit.

# Pyramid Peak The Trifecta

**14,018 feet** (39° 04' 18" N; 106° 57' 01" W)
**Bivy** July 29–30

Opposite: Sunset.
Right: Sunrise.

## Three Peaks in Three Consecutive Nights

In the middle of monsoon season, I never would have dreamed of knocking off the Maroon Bells and Pyramid Peak in three consecutive nights. On the afternoon of the 29th, I was in position to pull off the Elk Mountain Trifecta. I left the Maroon Lake parking lot at 4:30 p.m., making the summit just before 8:00 p.m. I had camped up on the summit the previous summer, so I knew exactly how much time it would take me to get up there with overnight gear, which proved to be a huge advantage for me this time around. I carried a little bit of food and some water to get me through the night after having a big afternoon meal at Aspen Highlands Village earlier.

Pyramid Peak should be placed on the list of the three most difficult fourteeners to climb, along with Capitol and Little Bear. It is a moderately technical challenge via either the northeast or northwest ridge routes. The rotten and brittle sedimentary shale follows a similar northeast orientation as the Maroon Bells. Add the steepness of the peak and a porphyritic intrusion on the south aspect of the northeast ridge to the equation and you have a recipe for disaster if the weather doesn't cooperate. What is even more amazing is that the mountain goats patrol the peak like a juvenile detention center! They follow you up the cliffs and try to snatch any of your gear, heavily drawn to the taste of salt that comes off your body. Beware of the rockfall from an unsuspecting goat anytime you tackle the great Pyramid.

**Meteorology**  We considered Pyramid Peak a routine summit to sleep on. Fast mountaineers can climb Pyramid Peak in four hours or less from the parking lot. Jon flew up Pyramid Peak, set up camp under clear skies, and had a great night of sleep. I had no weather worries.

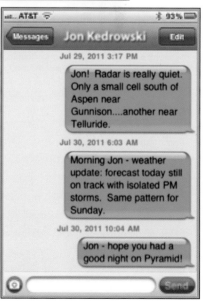

Jon Kedrowski

Jul 29, 2011 3:17 PM

Jon! Radar is really quiet. Only a small cell south of Aspen near Gunnison....another near Telluride.

Jul 30, 2011 6:03 AM

Morning Jon - weather update: forecast today still on track with isolated PM storms. Same pattern for Sunday.

Jul 30, 2011 10:04 AM

Jon - hope you had a good night on Pyramid!

Left: Drying out gear from overnight condensation in the warm morning sun with Snowmass and Capitol in the distance.

## Pyramid's Perch

The sedimentary layers are perfectly flat on the summit, and a perfectly sized platform was available for my tent right on the top. I faced the door to the southwest, and took advantage of light winds. As a safety precaution I piled some shale and slate blocks on the west side of the tent to remind myself not to go out that side because there was a 200-foot cliff within inches of my anchoring spot. This summit was no place to lose your mojo. I must say that the evening on Pyramid was one of the most satisfying and enjoyable bivys of the project due to the combination of views, good weather, and knowing that it was my third summit in three nights, and the fifth in six nights—a streak that has surely never before been experienced. The night was warm, calm, and the morning sunrise was stellar.

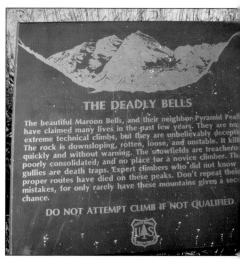

THE DEADLY BELLS

The beautiful Maroon Bells, and their neighbor Pyramid Peak, have claimed many lives in the past few years. They are no extreme technical climbs, but they are unbelievably deceptive. The rock is downsloping, rotten, loose, and unstable. It kills quickly and without warning. The snowfields are treacherous, poorly consolidated; and no place for a novice climber. The gullies are death traps. Expert climbers who did not know the proper routes have died on these peaks. Don't repeat their mistakes, for only rarely have these mountains given a second chance.

DO NOT ATTEMPT CLIMB IF NOT QUALIFIED

# Snowmass Mountain

## 21 Miles in 21 Hours

**14,092 feet** (39° 07' 08" N; 107° 03' 59" W)
**Bivy** August 22–23

Previous page: Sunset. Above: Hagerman Peak (left) and Snowmass Mountain (center) above Snowmass Lake.

... AT&T 93%

Messages   **Jon Kedrowski**   Edit

Aug 22, 2011 12:55 PM

Clouds building......10mins from snowmass th....plan is to get to lake by 4ish...eat, climb to summit from 5 to 7pm....up on the snowfield will try to call you before you go to bed.

Talk to you later!

Aug 22, 2011 6:10 PM

Storms are dying...you should be good Jon.

Aug 22, 2011 9:52 PM

Hey buddy....what do ya think?

summit at sunset....

Aug 23, 2011 4:45 AM

Very nice!! You nailed Snowmass!!!

Send

## A Long Trip Alone

The longest standard route approach and climb of a Colorado Fourteener on Monday evening and Tuesday morning kept me in the Elk Mountains and really tested my endurance. Snowmass Mountain isn't an incredibly difficult peak, but it is a long S.O.B.! You start at a low 8,400 feet at the Snowmass Falls trailhead and you make your way up Snowmass Creek for a long eight miles to Snowmass Lake at about 11,000 feet.

I started from the trailhead at 2:30 p.m., as I wanted to get an early enough start to "get into position" at the lake in the afternoon and head up the peak with enough time for storm delays of any kind.

The trail weaves through many aspen groves and can also be pretty awesome with fall colors come September. As I hiked up the trail I was rudely greeted by loud thunder cracking in the distance, so I remained on guard. Intermittent rain showers pelted me off and on for the eight miles to the lake. I kept my patience and hoped that skies would clear for the evening.

**Meteorology  Chris:** Snowmass is a tough customer because of the mileage from car to summit. It takes valuable energy to go the distance and my job was to identify a reliable weather window for Jon. I couldn't identify the perfect window, so Jon and I discussed strategies for a successful summit bivy. It came down to being smart, "getting into position," and operating incredibly fast and efficient.

The day Jon ascended Snowmass, a few afternoon thunderstorms developed right over the summit. Jon got into position at Snowmass Lake, watched the storms closely, and then made a speed ascent to the summit before sunset. Other climbers at Snowmass Lake watched Jon ascend in horror. But, this had become commonplace. We'd become exhibitionists on other peaks performing these late-day speed ascents. Jon hit the nail right on the head that night. Skies cleared and the satisfaction of succeeding on Snowmass on the first try is something I know Jon will never forget.

I arrived at the lake by 5:00 p.m. I was carrying very light gear, and only the essentials of food. Knowing that there would be water high on Snowmass, I kept my bottle and camelback nearly empty the entire hike in order to save weight.

After a few slices of elk sausage, an energy bar, and some water, I pressed on and into the Snowmass Lake willows. It had rained in the vicinity of the lake, so I received an unexpected shower from the amount of water left in the willows as I broke through them on the narrow lake trail. That was chilly! I made quick work of the scree slope below the famous "Snowmass" namesake snowfield of the peak. Late in August the snowfield was small and confined to areas on the final face of the peak from 13,300 to 13,800 feet. A few small rain showers stopped and moved to the east, just about the time I received a text from Chris telling me that it was all clear to the west and safe to go up.

## Barely Room for a Tent on Granite

I crested the ridge and raced up rubble and granite slabs and was at the summit by 7:20 p.m. I got the tent set up as fast as I could among the phaneritic boulders of the Snowmass Stock and shot the photos I needed in an incredibly clear night with a few high clouds on the horizon. Winds kept calm all evening and it felt good to know that all I had left to camp on in my favorite Elk Mountains was Capitol Peak, clearly visible and beckoning to the north.

Left: Early morning views—a long jagged ridge extending north for nearly five miles to Capitol Peak.

Snowmass Mountain,
Pierre Lakes Basin, and
Capitol Peak

# Colorado's Melting Snowpack, Climate Change, and the Dust Storm Phenomenon

The Pierre Lakes Basin is one of Colorado's most isolated and rugged watersheds. The basin is bordered on the north by Capitol Peak and on the south by Snowmass Mountain. In early spring 2009, a succession of five storm systems moved out of the Pacific Northwest and into the desert Southwest region of the United States. An early April storm system was the first storm of the series to entrain desert dust and deposit it onto the deep April snowpack of the Elk Mountains, specifically the Pierre Lakes Basin. SNOTEL (SNOw TELemetry) data from sites across the mountain ranges was examined to assess the rate of snowmelt, which was at least one month earlier than thirty-year historical records indicated in association with the storm-deposited dust.

In a recent scientific article,* we presented meteorological data, snow pack data, streamflow data, and repeat photography of the Pierre Lakes Basin during the summer months to demonstrate that the events of 2009 exhibited an earlier and accelerated rate of snowmelt from year-to-year changes in large-scale weather patterns. This includes radiative forcing by desert dust deposits as a snowmelt-contributing factor over prior years of the past decade, particularly 2005 and 1999. Just by chance, we happened to have photos from almost the same dates in August and September of 2009, 2005, and 1999. The visual impact likely from the darker dust increasing the rate of melt and lowering the albedo (reflectivity) of the snow is clearly seen in the series of photos taken by Jon from those years going back over a decade.

We decided to visit Capitol Peak during roughly the same dates in 2010 and 2011 to re-photograph the Pierre Lakes Basin. We found similar visual snowmelt trends taking place. These findings may indicate a continuing concern of a water crisis in the Colorado River Basin and water scarcity issues with increased population pressures in the southwestern United States for the coming decades.

* Kedrowski, J.J., Tomer, C.T. (2011). "Dirty Snow: Documenting the 2009 dust storm events in Colorado's San Juan and Elk Mountains with repeat photography and historical snowpack data." *NWA Online Electronic Journal of Operational Meteorology.* Nov 2010 EJ7. (1–39). http://www.nwas.org/ej/pdf/2010-EJ7.pdf

Opposite: This spectacular basin was once carved out by glaciers. Permanent snows are becoming more scarce every year by the end of summer, and especially noticeable in Pierre Lakes Basin.

# Capitol
# Peak Sharpening<br>the Knife Edge

**14,130 feet** (39° 09' 01" N; 107° 04' 59" W)
**Bivy** September 10–11

## Another Difficult Summit Bivy on the Third Attempt

The summer monsoon reared its ugly head on all three attempts of Capitol Peak. I've climbed the peak over a dozen times from both the northwest buttress (5.9, Grade IV) and the standard "Knife Edge" route (Class 4). The summer of 2011 felt like an unusually stormy summer, at least when I wanted to try camping on the summit of Capitol.

While getting into position on both July 30 and August 19, strong thunderstorms developed over the peak, and the 19th of August was especially discouraging as Chris and I were all the way up on the Knife Edge and about to cross it when radar confirmed that a huge storm was coming, which we observed developing to the west. We dropped off of Capitol just in the nick of time and decided to wait until September, our third attempt, when we were finally able to set up a tent on Capitol's scenic perch.

**Meteorology Chris:** Over the years I've noticed that Capitol Peak guards its summit with some of the worst weather of all the Elk Mountain 14ers, mainly due to its geographic position and jagged geometry. Inbound storms run right into the Capitol/Snowmass/Daly/Sopris granite walls. Prevailing wind is forced to rise abruptly in this area, and it's a collision zone of active weather.

We went to sleep under clearing skies, but awoke to freezing fog and near zero visibility. The wind was also blowing 20 to 30 mph. It was a bad combination on a tiny summit. Icy rock on Capitol Peak makes the Knife Edge traverse tricky. I was not expecting afternoon thunderstorms so we didn't have to rush, but if you find yourself shrouded in fog, be aware that fog may help contribute to widespread, earlier than normal afternoon thunderstorms. Fog is fairly common during the final days of the monsoon season. Colder air is trying to rush in from higher altitudes while lower levels are still incredibly moist from monsoon rains.

## Solid White Granite

In September, the weather was good enough to give us a weather window to make the summit bivy on Capitol. It was another classic sprint to the finish. At 4:30 p.m. we hiked up from Capitol Lake and positioned ourselves on K2. Storms from the afternoon cleared and moved to the east. Chris pushed me ahead across the Knife Edge so I could get the tent set up in time, while he waited for thirty minutes and monitored the radar—just in case. I'd been across the Knife Edge so many times that I think I could probably do it blindfolded. The white granite is solid for the most part for the majority of the route to the top.

Once on the summit, the fog and afternoon clouds—along with a dying storm to the west—left a unique scene upon the very narrow summit, where I managed to fit the tent right at the top next to the highest granite boulders. In the morning, residual late-season moisture fogged us in on the peak as we honored the tenth anniversary of the September 11th attacks.

Opposite: Third time is a charm. With summer fading we finally put a tent up on Capitol's rocky summit.

Above: Jon celebrating on the summit in early September 2005. Notice how much more snow was in the basin below Snowmass Mountain in 2005 compared to photos from 2011. Both years had similar snowfall totals the previous winter.

Right: Storms fading with the setting sun.

## Capitol Peak Geology: White Granite Giant Sculpted by Glaciers

An intersection of two separate joints created by uplift and then carved out by glaciers that formerly filled the valleys to the north and south have created the jagged northeast ridge of granite known as the Knife Edge. The curvature of the cirques of Pierre Lakes Basin and Capitol Lake have left behind only the most resistant white granite, which just happens to be along the northeast ridge of Capitol Peak and its exit point known as "Colorado's K2" (13,664 feet).

The Snowmass Stock of medium-grained granite is a 34-million-year-old uplift that intruded along the Elk Range thrust-fault, which further carried piles-upon-piles of regolith toward the southwest and also built the mountains extending toward Snowmass Mountain and the remainder of the granite peaks in the West Elk Mountains.

Irregular joints of various white granite composition give the peak its "columnar capitol building" resemblance, appropriate with the name of this striking 14,000-foot peak—considered one of Colorado's most challenging fourteener climbs.

**Meteorology   Pure Commitment:** The Knife Edge traverse across Capitol Peak requires a solid weather window of at least four hours. K2 is your decision point. The traverse from K2 to the summit and back is rigorous and time consuming. We were fortunate to have lots of experience on Capitol, so our window could be as little as two hours, but always know your own limits. Not only should you know the weather forecast, but you should be able to constantly diagnose the weather you see in the field.

We've traversed the Knife Edge in freezing fog, snow, ice, wind, and sunshine. The best days are in June and September. July and August feature daily afternoon thunderstorms, and successful summits in these months require efficiency and early Alpine starts. Most days start clear in the summer months. As the day progresses, you'll notice small cumulus clouds growing in size, then turning darker in color. This is the normal progression of afternoon thunderstorm development. During July and August this process happens more quickly because there's more moisture in the air to fuel these storms—called a monsoon. July and August thunderstorms are also wetter and more violent with frequent lightning and hail. While the wildflowers are stunning, the afternoon thunderstorms are killers.

*"We must not forget 9/11. We dedicate this bivouac of Colorado's most challenging fourteener to all Americans on 9/11/11."*

## 9/11 Tribute on Capitol Peak

I told Jon to use high altitude oven settings for the cinnamon rolls. It's tough baking at 14,130 feet with only an MSR Pocket Rocket. It was a sad state of affairs that morning as only one cinnamon roll rose to the occasion—the others stayed flat as pancakes. We ended up duking it out for that cinnamon roll while standing on the summit of what many consider Colorado's most challenging fourteener: Capitol Peak.

We rose from the ashes in our own way on the morning of 9/11/11. The mountain makes the decisions, and this was our third attempt to sleep on the tiny summit of Capitol Peak from sunset to sunrise. Booming thunderstorms had chased us off Capitol's Knife Edge twice before—but the third time was a charm. It goes to show that even a bonafide meteorologist can't control the weather.

I knew going in we'd be fighting weather forces. In one corner the seasonal monsoon, and in the other corner the cold fronts of September. As we arrived at K2 on the evening of 9/10/11 my watch read 6:30 p.m. I knew from my weathercast earlier that morning that the sun was going set at 7:17 p.m. This meant we had under an hour to traverse the Knife Edge, reach the summit, and set up camp before sunset. To achieve this we performed a speed ascent in the wake of dying afternoon thunderstorms. I watched the radar closely and kept giving Jon the green light, which consisted of me waiving my red hat like a loon. The Knife Edge was a blur as we raced across. We set up our summit camp, snapped high-resolution sunset photos, and reminisced about where we were just ten years prior on 9/11/01.

It was 9/11/01 and we were roommates living in a Valparaiso, Indiana, apartment. I was starting my senior year at Valparaiso University majoring in Meteorology, and Jon was majoring in Mountain Geography and would later earn a Ph.D. Little did we know that ten years later we would combine our skills to accomplish this first-ever fourteeners feat. We had both just finished basketball practice when we heard the tragic news. It was almost as if time stood still that morning.

Ten years later we awoke to freezing fog, 30 mph wind gusts, and temperatures in the teens. Winter was moving in. Without saying a word, we both knew the significance of that morning. I grabbed my camera and began snapping photos of a red sunrise across the rooftop of Colorado. Rays of morning sun bounced through the thick fog. We both felt patriotic—this was freedom.

Capitol's summit is tiny and uncomfortable for an overnight bivy, but when you gaze across the Elk Mountains—from the Maroon Bells to Snowmass Mountain and down into Pierre Lakes Basin—you forget about how little you've slept. The bigger picture emerged on that small summit. Our friendship is solid—we're still dreaming big, eating cinnamon rolls, climbing mountains, and trying to make a difference. Our story is about teamwork, about climbing the proverbial mountain together. Members of both our families served in the military. We dedicate our accomplishment to them and to all Americans.

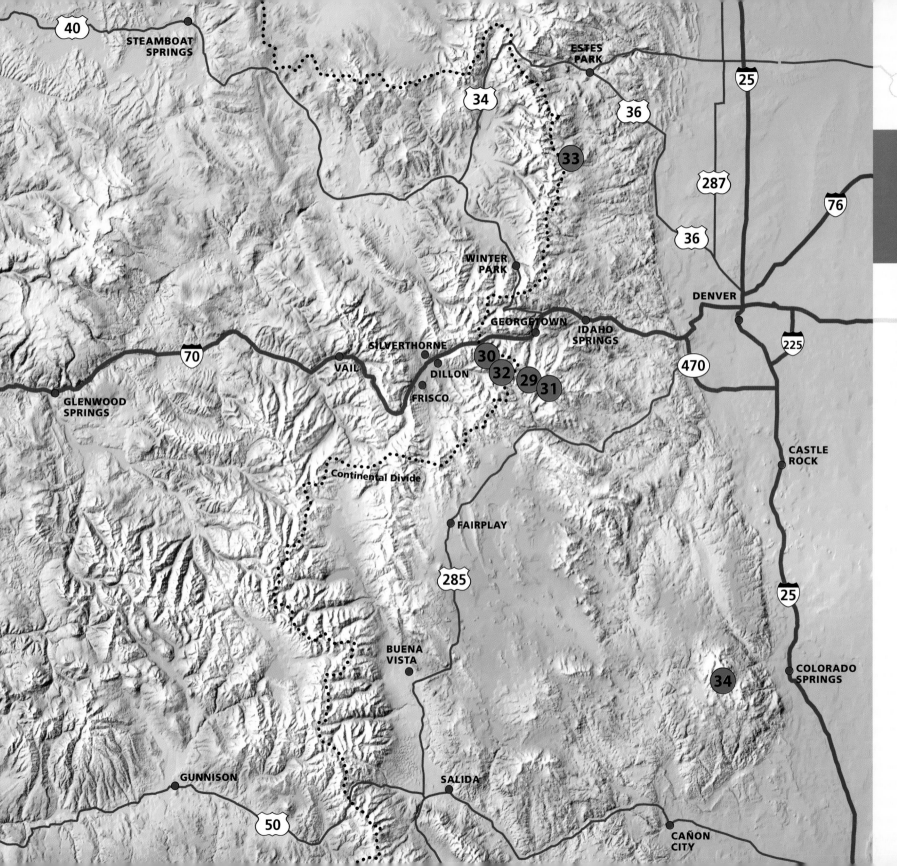

# Mount Bierstadt

## Get me a Bier, "Stadt"!

**14,060 feet** (39° 34' 57" N; 105° 40' 08" W)
**Bivy** July 31–August 1

## Most Popular Range in Colorado

After a burnout of five peaks in six nights and quite an impressive streak over in the Elks, I decided to turn my attention to the Front Range. The six peaks of the Front Range are the most heavily trodden fourteeners in all of Colorado. With nearly four million people in cities and towns along the Denver metropolitan urban corridor, it makes sense. Most of the trailheads start at higher elevations, and most of the standard routes are easy walk-ups. These reasons make the Front Range peaks a popular outdoor activity for people looking for their first fourteener experience. If you're looking to camp on a summit for the first time, a Front Range peak may be the ideal setup for you.

After a short rest at home in Vail, I decided to make use of my time and location to climb an easy peak close to Denver—or so I thought! I found my way up to the Guanella Pass trailhead and the infamous Bierstadt Meadows leading toward the peak at about 6:00 p.m. I thought Bierstadt would be a walk in the park. I knew from past climbs that I could make it up Bierstadt in an hour and a half, even with overnight gear. But the weather had other plans. I was all set to head up the peak when a nasty lightning storm engulfed the entire mountain range. To make matters worse, I was slammed by a storm while parked at the pass, which meant I would really be short on time in order to make the summit before sunset. The storm especially raged over the peaks to the east of Bierstadt, which gave me a glimmer of hope that they would move off quickly.

Opposite: A grey sunset from fading evening storms.

Right: Storms still rage out over the eastern plains after dark.

Left: View to the west in the early morning light.

In closer consultation with Chris over the phone, he assured me that the storms would move out by 6:45 p.m.—I would be forced to make another speed ascent. I went as light as I could, burned my lungs out putting the hammer down, and arrived up on Bierstadt's summit just before 8:00 p.m.

## A Rocky Magnetic Sawtooth

The summit is extremely rocky with hardly any spaces that are flat enough for a tent. I quickly moved some pretty large granite and biotite boulders to make room.

In 1863, magnetite rocks were supposedly the reason that Alfred Bierstadt became slightly disoriented in his first ascent while using his compass near the summit to orient himself with his position among these peaks in the Front Range. To the east is the glacially carved granite connecting ridge between Bierstadt and Mount Evans, known as the Sawtooth. This scenic ridge connecting the two peaks is the 1.4-billion-year-old Mount Evans Batholith.

**Meteorology Chris:** We considered Bierstadt an "easy" summit bivy. Fast hikers can reach its summit in under two hours. Jon gave me his itinerary and I gave him the weather forecast. I knew afternoon thunderstorms were likely. The monsoon was in full swing to further aid in the development of storms. I felt like it was going to be a nasty mix. In spite of that, I knew Jon could wait out most of the storms before starting his ascent. That's exactly how it played out, too. Jon waited in his truck until an hour before sunset, grabbed his gear and proceeded to perform a speed ascent. He arrived on the summit just as the thunderstorms pushed east.

Above: Looking back to Guanella Pass as the sunlight shines through after the storms before sunset. Inset: The Sawtooth is obvious to the left of the summit of Bierstadt in this photo.

# Grays Peak

## Highest Point on the Continental Divide

**14,270 feet** (39° 38' 02" N; 105° 49' 03" W)
**Bivy** August 1–2

Above: A cloudy evening on divide. Below: Early morning fog to the north, Torreys Peak in view.

Sunrise.

Opposite: Grays (left) and Torreys (right)—brilliant wildflowers in upper Stevens Basin.

## Going Green on Grays

I had to hurry once again to make it to the summit to capture the stormy sunset photos. Fortunately, on that night I had better weather and a little extra time. After visiting Chris in Golden and getting an up-to-date forecast, I headed for the Grays Peak trailhead off of I-70 at Bakerville.

The clock read 6:00 p.m. as I pulled into the trailhead. I packed my gear, including my tent, 15-degree down sleeping bag, and new down hoody. Leaving the Grays trailhead at about 6:30 p.m., I hustled up the peak. On the northeast face of Grays at 13,500 feet, there were some more goats. I also got some glimpses to the east, looking at Bierstadt and Evans, which both had storms raging. A quick check of my text messages revealed a weather update from Chris. He said that all the storm systems were tracking to the northeast, so I had nothing to worry about. Only some thick fog to my west, and by 7:45 p.m., I made the summit of Grays in only an hour and fifteen minutes!

## Front Range Summit on the Divide

I gave the famous blue tent the night off for the first time in years, and tried out a brand new one that weighs about a pound. By 8:00 p.m. I was all set up and shooting sunset photos. The air was crisp and cool, and the winds were pretty light. Grays is the highest peak in the Front Range. The summit is narrow but long, with plenty of room for a tent behind the massive summit rock wall—built over time by the thousands of people that climb the mountain every summer. It's hard to imagine what the summit would've looked like in 1861 when the first recorded ascent took place by Charles C. Perry, a Denver area botanist. Mr. Perry supposedly named it for his secret lover and botanist colleague, Asa Gray. Clearly, the excessive social trail system and scattered energy bar wrappers would not have been seen here way back then. Grays Peak could have also derived its name from the piles of grey biotite, gneiss, and schist, including the grey streaky migmatite that was uplifted to the highest point on North America's Continental Divide during the Laramide Orogeny.

**Meteorology** Chris: Grays and Torreys required two nights, making two incredibly easy peaks a much more difficult circumstance. Jon chose to do each peak individually in two separate "dash and crash" events. This was the best idea considering the unpredictable nature of the monsoon, and the fact that these peaks were barely over an hour to the summit and only an hour back to the trailhead each morning. There was residual moisture on Grays, but storms moved out early, so Jon had this one in the bag. Torreys would prove to be much more of a hassle later in the week.

# Mount Evans

## Project Half-way Point

**14,264 feet** (39° 35' 018" N; 105° 38' 38" W)
**Bivy** August 3–4

Right: Sunset facing toward Denver. The highest summit
block was just large enough for a tent. Summit Lake
(lower left), observatory parking lot (lower right).

**Meteorology** I went to bed around 10:00 p.m. and was hit by a small rogue storm out of the south. Fortunately the lightning was minimal, and I didn't have to retreat to the safety of my truck. By midnight the rain was over and I slept soundly until 5:00 a.m., when I was up for the sunrise and my morning commute down to Idaho Springs!

**Chris:** We considered Mount Evans the easiest summit bivy of them all, along with Pikes Peak. Jon wanted to keep Evans in his back pocket as an option for a night of bad weather. In the end, Jon completed Evans as dozens of curious on-lookers questioned his tent on the summit block.

Above: Sunrise over Summit Lake and the northern Front Range.

Left: The lights of the Denver metropolitan corridor in the distance (photo by Eric George).

Summit Lake.

## Highest Paved Road in North America

I decided to celebrate the halfway point of the project by taking it easy up on Mt. Evans. I have climbed the peak about ten times, and skied from its summit in the wintertime. In all my life, I had never driven up to the summit parking lot. I let the truck do most of the work as I drove to the top on North America's highest paved road, completed originally in the late 1920s. I relished the "day off" so to speak, in order to "sleep on the top of all Colorado fourteeners."

I'd slept on twenty-nine peaks and had twenty-nine more to do. Since I am a former college basketball athlete, we'll call it halftime. I felt great, I'd had tons of fun, and most importantly, I hadn't gotten hurt or killed yet. But honestly, besides the storms on Sunlight and Windom, and the awful weather on Torreys Peak the previous night in a failed attempt, I had been very fortunate.

## Mt. Evans Batholith

From the parking lot I still had to hike up the last 200 feet about five times for various reasons (bathroom, food, sleeping bag, gear, etc). It was a busy day on the summit, including making some new friends (photographers and baby goats!).

At 4:30 p.m. I arrived on the summit, and set up the tent on one of the highest summit blocks. Two observations were made: 1) Many of the onlookers were wondering what the heck I was doing up on that block with my tent, and 2) It was very difficult to find any loose rocks to help anchor the tent on that summit. Tourists over the years have removed most of the loose rocks as souvenirs.

The 1.4-billion-year-old Mount Evans Batholith dominates the summit. The entire peak is darker solid granite, with biotite streaks. The angular blocks of granite are oriented in a moderately inclined fashion from east to west and face steeply north. Magnetite is also present here, as are brilliantly carved glacial cirques, especially directly off the north summit face and down to Summit Lake and the Chicago Lakes Basin. Glaciers no longer exist here, but at one time they stretched into at least seven of the valleys extending out from Mount Evans and all the way to Denver, thirty-six miles away, to the foot of the state capitol building. Most days you can see downtown Denver, and tonight the evening skyline of the Denver metropolitan area was illuminated after sunset and accented with nighttime thunderstorm activity over the eastern plains.

Opposite: Eastern skies illuminated by the fading sunset.

# Torreys Peak Grays' Evil Stepsister

**14,267 feet** (39° 38' 34" N; 105° 49' 16" W)
**Bivy** August 4–5

The tent was set up quickly after the storm passed.

## Second Bivy Attempt in Three Days

Torreys is only three feet lower than Grays and proved to be "Grays' Evil Stepsister." Despite a stormy failure on Torreys on August 2, I had made the summit on that night. However, I still had to camp up there and also get some good sunset and sunrise photos for the project. It turned out that I couldn't get my tent up in the bad weather on August 2, so I retreated down the mountain. Wednesday was a night on Evans, and then I returned to Torreys for Thursday (August 4) with a much-improved forecast from Chris. I decided to start a bit earlier (4:00 p.m.) from the Stephen's Gulch trailhead above Bakerville. This allowed me to get into a better position to wait out any sort of bad weather or waves of rain and hail that might move through.

Torreys takes a little longer to hike than Grays because you have to go up Gray's face, traverse the face to the saddle and head up the southeast ridge. This time I took a forty-minute break at 13,200 feet at the base of Grays face because I had cell service. Chris indicated that there was a line of storms moving through (which I knew because I was getting rained on), and that I should be able to go for the top in a weather window right after the storm passed. This time Chris was spot on. At 5:30 p.m. the sun came out, and I waltzed to the summit under partly cloudy skies by 6:15 p.m.

**Meteorology** **Chris:** A couple of years ago we did a speed ascent to the summit of Torreys Peak in roughly an hour, so we both knew how long it would take to climb from the trailhead to the summit. I told Jon that afternoon thunderstorms were likely, and in the case of Torreys Peak, the storms may last into the night. I kept Jon updated with real-time storm information. Jon nailed Torreys Peak both times he climbed to stay up there, but the afternoon storms did indeed last into the night keeping him from the summit bivy on the first try. He got it on try two with a weather window and just a little bit of hail that came through once he was safely in his tent.

Above: High lenticular saucer cloud above Grays in the early morning.
Right: Greeted by goats during 2005 summit bivy.

## Tiny Torreys Summit

I had previously camped on Torreys Peak before heading to Elbrus in Russia in 2005. The immediate summit area is only about the size of half a basketball court. The nearly 35-million-year-old Montezuma Stock of gneiss, schist, and porphyry granite rocks and cairns have been moved around every year by the thousands that hike to the summit of Torreys. I tried putting my tent down on the spot nearest to where I had camped in 2005, to see what kind of repeat photos I could get. This year's photos would have a new green tent; my 2005 photos sported the classic blue tent.

By 7:30 p.m. I was settled into my tent and getting a last forecast from Chris. I saw a few large clouds to the west that were coming my way fast, but otherwise things were pretty quiet. After a dinner of sandwiches and hot chocolate, I heard some loud pellets of hail and graupel pelting the tent. I peered outside to a brief whiteout of hail, but it only lasted a few minutes. Once the storm passed the residual clouds made for a really cool backdrop to the sunset.

# Longs Peak Through the Cracks

**14,259 feet** (40° 15' 18" N; 105° 36' 54" W)
**Bivy** August 5–6

### Front Range Giant: Colorado's Northernmost Fourteener

I am sure that people have camped on the summit of Longs Peak, but the National Park Service doesn't even issue permits for its incredibly spacious summit. You usually have to camp in a bivy site on a rock route or use the Boulder Field. Of the three previous times I'd climbed Longs in 1996, 2002, and 2005, I'd never even seen a ranger patrolling the standard route. However, due to the high volume of climbers attempting the peak, there are usually NPS rangers in the area.

"Nobody is going to be up there, especially not in the afternoon. All we need is good weather and we are golden," I told Chris.

Above: Chris enjoying the early morning solitude. Right: Jon approaching the Keyhole, the point of no return.

Our plan was to go fast, light, and efficient with only overnight gear and a Steripen to filter water and fill our bottles just below the Keyhole. Into our packs also went four slices of Papa John's pizza each, a few select energy bars of choice, peanut butter and jelly sandwiches for the descent, along with a Red-Bull, a deck of mini-playing cards, and no stove. We were good to go.

## Climbed By Thousands

Longs Peak is climbed more often than any other fourteener in Colorado. My research since 2005 indicates that more than 10,000 people attempt Longs annually, while only about half make it to the summit according to park rangers. The close proximity to Denver, the convenient location in a national park, and the delightful light-grey solid granite of Longs are all good reasons for the high climbing frequency. The ease of accessibility can be a concern. People often underestimate the fifteen-mile round trip journey and the moderately difficult scramble on the mountain's upper portions. Dozens of rescues occur every year because of these factors. Don't be the next statistic on Longs. Bring appropriate gear and start early so that afternoon storms don't ruin your day or place your life at risk.

Longs Peak and its nearby neighbor—Mount Meeker—are part of the 1.4 billion-year-old Longs Peak–St. Vrain Batholith, one of Colorado's oldest mountain range complexes. The granite has a number of near-vertical joints with igneous intrusions of potassium feldspar, including metamorphic evidence in the biotite schist and migmatite slabs.

**Meteorology  Chris:** Longs Peak requires nearly perfect weather for an afternoon approach and overnight bivy. I closely watched the weather for a couple of weeks prior to our bivy, waiting for just the right break in the monsoon. There's no quick retreat from the summit of Longs when the rock is wet.

Longs is also notorious for its wind. Gusts to over 200 mph are not uncommon in winter, and there can be gusts of 100 mph in the summer, with 70 mph sustained winds a commonality.

Climber's weather tip: Don't get summit fever! Diagnose the prevailing weather at the Keyhole before committing to the summit.

Left: Traversing the narrow ledges toward the trough along the east side of the peak. Painted bulls-eyes mark the path of least resistance.

Opposite: Storms fade to the northwest as the sun sets.

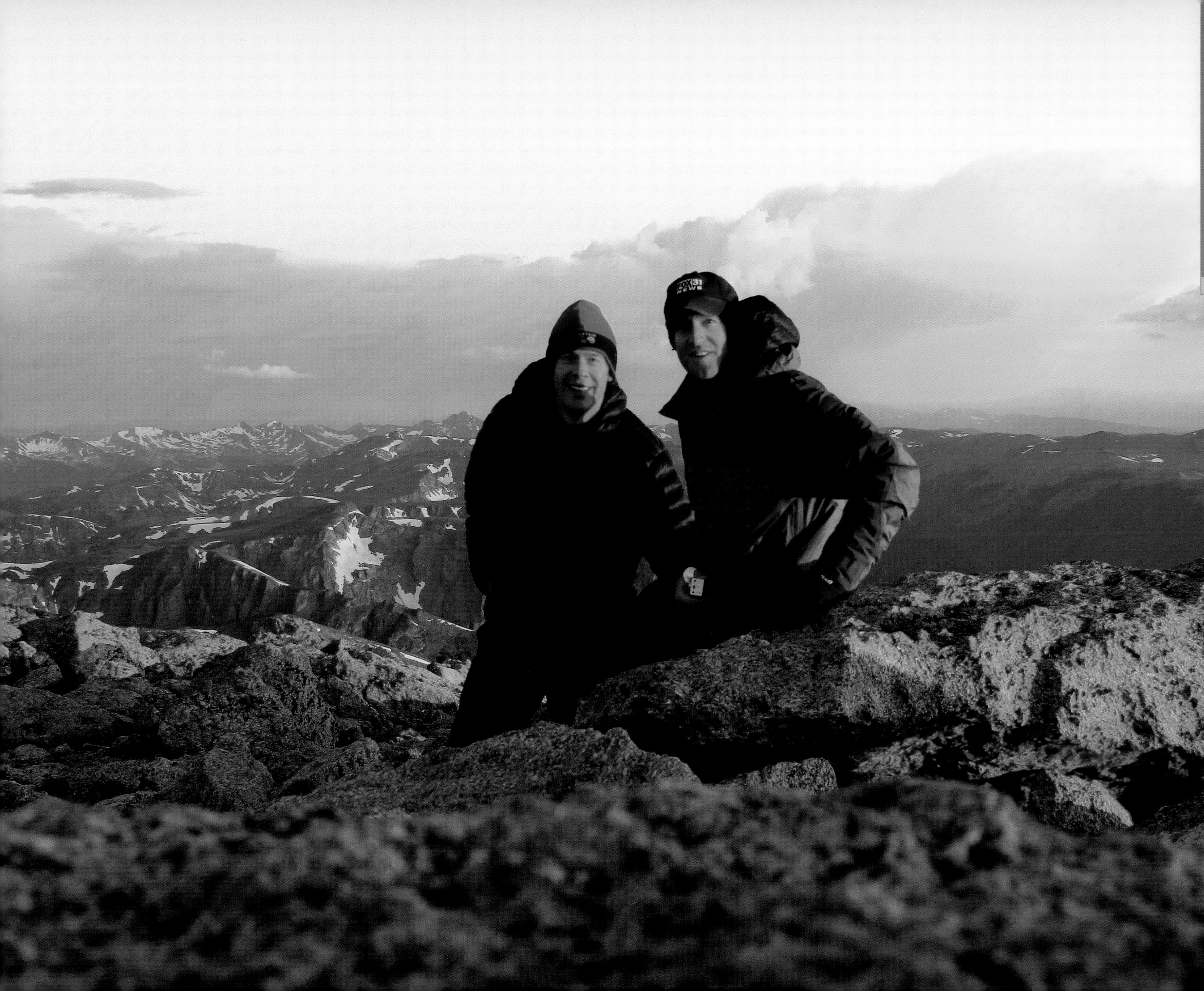
FOX 31
NEWS

# Pikes Peak

## America the Beautiful

**14,111 feet** (38° 50' 26" N; 105° 02' 39" W)
**Bivy** August 6–7

### Easternmost Colorado Fourteener by Cog Railway

I caught the last train of the day at 5:20 p.m. Saturday in the sweltering afternoon heat of Manitou Springs. Temperature was in the 90s and I looked a bit foolish among all the tourists with my large backpack, down jacket, warm clothes, and overnight gear. The train rushed skyward, into the lush forests of ponderosa pine and quaking aspen, and within forty-five minutes we were already above the timber and the cool mountain breezes pushed us toward the summit. There were a few storms in the area, although Chris assured me there would be nothing major. Most of the time he is right, yet I had heard the same thing earlier in the week when I had to abort staying on Torreys Peak, even though I had made the summit easily in the awful weather. Forecasts and radar were a great asset to this project, although I will still caution everyone out there who ventures into the mountains: Knowing the forecast is no substitute for preparation and assessing weather and route conditions in the field.

### Most Visited Colorado Fourteener Summit

The summit of Pikes is huge. It rivals Bross in size, flatness, and area. It is larger than Longs, but 150 feet lower. The parking lot circles the highest point, a pile of rocks with no significant markings of any kind. The 1-billion-year-old

Sunrise; the restaurant provided excellent wind protection.

pink Pikes Peak granite is primarily composed of potassium feldspar. This igneous rock exhibits large pink and orange crystals created by gradual magma cooling over time, rivaling the feldspar seen in the San Juans on Mount Eolus.

By 7:30, the last train of the day left, and the highway ranger patrols had finally booted the last cars down the road. It was only me and a few staff members remaining at the restaurant. The hail had subsided for a moment. I decided to set up the tent on the north side of the main building to use it as a wind shield. The new tent was easy to set up, and by 8:00 p.m. I was getting all the excellent sunset photos I needed on the most civilized and iconically sold Colorado Fourteener peak ever. A gust of wind and a few lightning strikes kept me on guard just prior to midnight. At one point I had to re-anchor my tent in a brief squall, but I used the large restaurant shelter to my advantage that evening.

**Meteorology  Chris:** We were entering a fairly dry stretch when Jon slept on the summit of Pikes Peak. However, there was one fly in the ointment. The forecast models for three days straight kept showing a late-day thunderstorm developing over South Park and moving quickly toward Pikes Peak then out over the eastern plains of Colorado. This was not a monsoon-driven pattern, and with drier air now at higher levels of the atmosphere I knew the potential was there for a high wind event. Jon texted and called me with news of dark clouds brewing near Pikes Peak and immediately I knew the stormy scenario was going to materialize.

Pikes Peak marks a very sharp cutoff from high mountains to lower elevation flat ranchlands. We're talking an 8,000-foot vertical drop into Colorado Springs. Wind events are common, and intense Chinook heating, severe thunderstorms, and even tornadoes can spin-up in this area. Summer high temperatures can be in the thirties on the summit, while being close to a hundred in Colorado Springs. This temperature range creates intense pressure gradients driving the entire process.

Sunset.

Pikes Peak Cog Railroad, highest railway in North America.

# Pikes Peak: Selling Colorado Through History and an Iconic Fourteener

In 1806, Pikes Peak was first sighted by members of Zebulon Pike's expedition. They attempted to climb the mountain, but failed due to deep snow, extreme cold, and lack of provisions. The mountain wasn't climbed until 1820 by Edwin James, a botanist and member of Stephen Long's expedition.

In 1893, Katherine Lee Bates wrote words to the famous anthem "America the Beautiful" from the summit. There is a monument commemorating this on the eastern end of the summit.

Today's version of Pikes Peak's summit is a far cry from the original. They say that Pikes Peak is the second most visited summit in the world behind Mount Fuji in Japan. Nearly 250,000 people per year make it up Pikes, 95 percent using cars or the cog railroad.

On Pikes there is enough room to hold a train depot, large viewing deck, a handful of monuments, a restaurant, gift shop, U.S. Army weather station, and N.O.A.A weather station. Even with all that stuff up there you could still have room for a smaller version of Folsom Field in Boulder on the top. The parking lot is huge, and the newly paved Pikes Peak highway ends at the restaurant and gift shop.

Playing tourist for this particular summit bivy was enjoyable, and in the morning I had taken my tent down before the 9:00 a.m. train arrived from Manitou Springs. I entered the restaurant and enjoyed fresh baked doughnuts and hot chocolate before departing the summit via train down into the warm summer day in the valleys below. While on the train, it really started to dawn on me that I only had to finish the peaks in the Sangre de Cristos and Sawatch Range, as well as Capitol Peak, in order to complete the entire project.

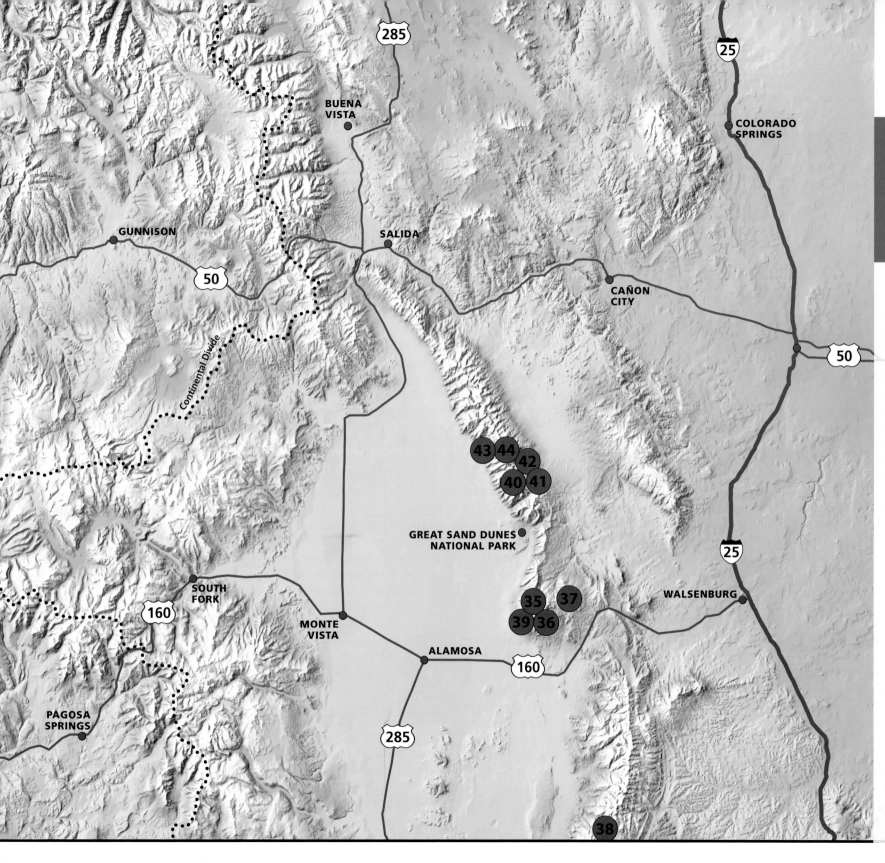

# Sangre de Cristo Range
Unforgettable Adversity

# Ellingwood Point

Change of Plans

**14,042 feet** (37° 34' 57" N; 105° 29' 33" W)
**Bivy** August 25–26

Above: Sunrise, with Mount Lindsey in the distance. Below: Stormy sunset over the San Luis Valley.

# Sprint to the Summit

I wanted to do the toughest peak first. I started up Little Bear but at the top of the "v-notch" couloir, the dark and ominous clouds were everywhere. A loud boom from the southeast was part of a huge storm cloud developing. I quickly got on the phone with Chris to see if there would be any chance for me to ascend. He confirmed what I saw standing at 12,500 feet. A thunderstorm cluster was sliding out of the San Luis Valley directly into Little Bear. I knew this was not going to be my night to sleep on Little Bear's summit—I'd have to resort to "Plan B." "Maybe I can go down to base camp really fast and head up Ellingwood if the storms clear out," I said to Chris as I started to get pelted by graupel. It was approaching 6:00 p.m. and I had to make a decision. There was no way I could go up Little Bear in those conditions. "The storms should clear out by 7:00 or 7:30 p.m.," Chris replied. But this setup reminded me of Capitol Peak only a week earlier. I couldn't proceed any farther and my sunset window was closing. It was late August and sunset wasn't at 8:30 p.m. like it is in late June or early July. I only had until 7:45 p.m. that day to make the summit.

At that point I completely switched gears mentally and decided to abort Little Bear and go for Ellingwood Point. At least if I was in the basin by 6:30, I could conceivably hike in rain, and then hope for the rain to stop as I neared the summit for the final Class 2+ scree scramble by 7:30 p.m. It was worth a shot. I was still fresh from a few days off. "I'm

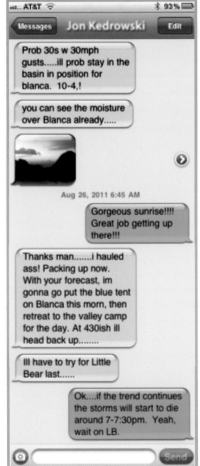

A small notch just west of the true summit provided a great tent platform.

Ellingwood Point (center) keeps watch over the Upper Como Basin.

going to go down Chris, and go for Ellingwood." Chris told me, "I'll keep you updated and send you a text at sevenish. You should be in good shape by the time you hit the final summit ridge. By then, I think the skies will be clearing."

I didn't have a minute to lose. I was sliding down dirt and scree in the pouring hail and rain, but I didn't care. I had to make it to Ellingwood Point. This project depended on it. I wasn't going to stay in the Lake Como Basin, worried about ravenous bears, and I couldn't afford to get stuck trying to do these peaks for another day, when I still had nineteen others to do.

In a flash I was back to my base camp where the green tent was set up. I grabbed one trekking pole from my tent, and kept on going. By 6:45 the rain had stopped and it appeared it was starting to diminish for the night. Conditions were really wet, so it would have been a challenge to get up the technical sections of Little Bear. I passed two people hanging out at a small lake in the upper basin at about ten minutes to seven. No time to talk, so I pushed on. A little fog over the peaks of Blanca and Ellingwood, but that didn't worry me as I hadn't heard any thunder in about thirty minutes. By 7:15 I was in the saddle between Blanca and Ellingwood. After a quick sip of water, I powered up the last 400 vertical feet on large boulders and scree, arriving on the summit at 7:30 p.m.

## Albert Ellingwood's Perch

Elation! I had made it! The sun was going down behind some clouds and I quickly set up my blue tent among the green horneblende and gabbro. This sub-summit of the Blanca Massif was named for one of Colorado's mountaineering pioneers, Sir Albert Ellingwood, who was one of the first to climb all of the fourteeners. By 7:40 p.m. I was snapping photos in 30 mph winds, and I couldn't believe it! For me to go from the v-notch over on Little Bear, all the way up to Ellingwood Point in an hour and a half was unreal! It was a true speed ascent and I still felt good.

It was a windy night, but I didn't care. Even with all the wind, I fell asleep fast, feeling thrilled that I only had nineteen more nights to go on Colorado Fourteener summits.

Opposite: A dark and stormy evening.

# Blanca
# Peak Strategy in the Sangres

**14,345 feet** (37° 34' 38" N; 105° 29' 09" W)
**Bivy** August 26–27

## Highest Peak in the Sangre de Cristos

I departed Ellingwood's summit in the warm morning sunshine. To save some critical time and weight later in the day, I chose to quickly climb up Blanca with the tent, secure it and then retreat to the basin to my "day camp" to rest for the day, eat, and wait out storms. This step in getting my tent placed on the summit would prove to be the difference between success and failure on Blanca later that evening.

Later that day when I was heading back up, things weren't looking good at all, in fact they were getting worse. Around 5:45 p.m., lightning was striking all over the place in the basin to the west, and it was coming straight at me. It was a spectacular show, and the thunder shook the entire valley. I continued on up into the basin to 12,700 feet. Suddenly, my cell phone vibrated to life with a couple of updates from Chris.

His text message read, "Storms weakening ... You should be in great shape by 7–7:30."

His assessment was comforting, yet the rain to the west wasn't letting up—it was still pouring. I got rattled by a few lightning strikes and stopped and waited. Six o'clock came and went, then 6:15, and it continued to rain. I held my ground. Another message from Chris: "Clearing to the west of you."

Above: Sunrise.

Top: Sunset obscured by the rain and snow showers.

Right: Sunrise colors and Little Bear's jagged summit seen to the right of the tent.

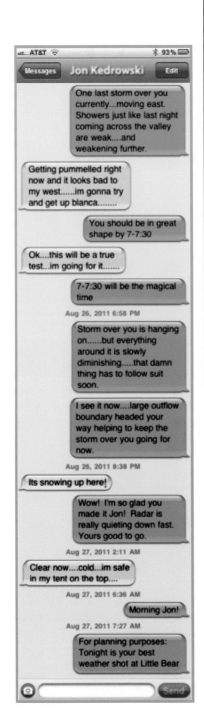

Despite the continuing lightning, I had faith in the forecasted clearing and the plan was executed. I pushed on and ascended Blanca in the pouring rain. The trail faded near some small cliffs at 13,400 feet; it had been raining so much the entire afternoon that the cliffs were waterfalls! I hustled up that section, cruised over some boulders, and gained the ridgeline at 13,800 feet. A quick glance to the west revealed a wall of clouds coming, as the westerly basins were still receiving downpours.

Bighorn sheep in the Upper Como Basin could sense the approaching storm as Jon climbed Blanca.

## Sacred Navajo Mountain of the East

At 7:30 p.m. I reached the summit in pouring rain, but the lightning had subsided. My previously pitched tent amid the greenish gabbro and dark 1.8-billion-year-old granite provided the shelter I needed in that crisis, and also saved me the valuable time I needed to get the photos before it became too dark. Before I could retire to my tent for the evening, snow flurries started to fall. The seasons were starting to change and I still had eighteen peaks to go.

Blanca is the highest peak in the Sangre de Cristos and the fourth highest peak in Colorado. The Navajo Indians consider it a sacred mountain, and there were Indian sacrifices and burnings found in a small stone structure on its summit by members of the Wheeler Survey in 1874. I surely wasn't the first person to spend the night up there.

**Meteorology** **Chris:** I remember talking with Jon about the storm potential on the fourteeners surrounding Lake Como. I was watching the radar closely for several days and the Sierra Blanca Massif was forcing strong thunderstorm development every day, lasting until 7:00 p.m. Jon watched the skies closely and took advantage of every weather window. Unfortunately, the windows were small and Jon was forced to perform speed ascents on both Ellingwood and Blanca to make the summits before sunset. The storms were so strong the evening of Jon's bivy on Blanca that they pulled down colder air from higher levels within the atmosphere and the precipitation ended as snowfall.

# Mount
# Lindsey Old Baldy

**14,042 feet** (37° 35' 01" N; 105° 26' 42" W)
**Bivy** August 29–30

Top: Sunset among the distant storm clouds and the Blanca Massif. Above: Sunrise.

The Iron Nipple (left) and Blanca (right) greets you deep inside the Huerfano River Valley.

## Getting My Mojo Back

On the night of August 27, my truck was ransacked by a voracious bear while I was on Blanca. I had been chased off by storms twice on Little Bear, and I was battered from two days of nasty thunderstorms while ascending Ellingwood and Blanca. Add to the mix the bear ate most of my stored food and busted out my passenger-side window. The bear break-in would eventually cost me a few hundred dollars in damage, not to mention lost time. Times were tough, yet I kept a strong positive mindset. We always have to realize that we cannot control things that have happened in the past or the very immediate present. We can only move forward and look to the future and the new opportunities. I was determined to succeed. Instead of waiting in Alamosa for a new window in my truck and for the project to pass me by, I decided to climb Mount Lindsey, which stands alone to the east of the Blanca Massif.

As I headed to the trailhead for Lindsey, I recalled sitting in Alamosa the day before and closely watching one of the largest and nastiest thunderstorms of the entire summer pound the southern Sangre de Cristos all afternoon. The evidence was still in the Huerfano River Valley—deep piles of hail from the day before, broken tree limbs, and deeply cut stream washouts of mud and debris on the dirt access road. It rained during my entire two-hour drive from Alamosa to the trailhead. My chance to climb Lindsey looked bleak, yet I still believed I could make it up to the top for the night.

At 5:00 p.m. I arrived at the trailhead, and thankfully, the rain suddenly stopped. I moved with anxiousness and efficiency. This ascent up Lindsey was a classic example of my "dash and crash" strategy that I had perfected throughout this project. I was carrying only my lightweight overnight bivy gear and just enough food and water to survive the night.

At 6:30 p.m. I was on the high saddle about to scramble up Lindsey's north face. By good fortune, the sun was out and the winds were light. I gained the summit ridge and waltzed to the small rock shelter on the summit right at 7:00 p.m. In only about two hours from the trailhead, I had reached the summit in good weather! Number forty-one was complete.

## Tent on Tonolite

A large thunderstorm was brewing to the southeast, roughly sixty miles away on the plains of Colorado as I set up my tent on the fine-grained igneous intrusive rock known as tonolite, which dominates the summit. I had plenty of time to spare once I got my tent up, so I enjoyed the elk sausage and jerky that I had brought up with me, as well as the sugar snap peas and peanut butter and jelly sandwiches. I took a moment to sterilize the liter of water I had grabbed at the last spring-fed stream at tree line. I used some of the plagioclase feldspar, quartz, and tonolite rocks to anchor my tent as the evening winds intensified. I shot a few nifty pictures of the remaining storms in just about every direction, but I could tell they weren't headed my way. It was safe to stay and enjoy my night with Lindsey.

**Meteorology  Chris:** Lindsey was alive with storms the entire afternoon until about 5:00 p.m., when Jon started his speed ascent of the peak. There was activity in all directions, but Jon was fortunate to stay in a window of storm-free activity on Lindsey's summit as time passed that night. Winds were strong that evening due to so many storms in all directions and changing pressure gradients between the storms, which often increase wind speeds.

As a rule of thumb, the Sangre de Cristos require extreme caution during the monsoon months of July and August. Rich moisture flows up from the south adding fuel to the normal development of afternoon thunderstorms. The intense vertical rise of the Sangres adds to the violent nature of these thunderstorms. Why? Air is forced to rise more rapidly from the San Luis Valley up to the summits of these 14ers. In most cases we're talking almost an 8,000-foot vertical rising motion within these developing thunderstorms. These storms reflect the violent nature of the ascending air.

---

*Text messages:*

**Jon Kedrowski**

Well, thanks man, but i think speed helped a lot......and storms were off Lindsey after430....I left at 515 and made the summit at 7! Im so fast and fit now...its amazing!

That's amazing speed! And thank God the storms diminished early today. Both Tuesday PM and Wednesday PM still look drier.

Aug 29, 2011 9:15 PM

Yesterday the thunderoud over this whole area was catastrophic and enormous! And when i drove through to Lindsey trailhead, there were 6inch piles of hail stil in the woods....lots of flooding too the remnants....

Tomorrows plan....get iff here by 7am, back to the car by 9 back to alamosa

Aug 29, 2011 10:10 PM

Peak #41 Mt. Lindsey, made it up tonight after a storm!

Aug 30, 2011 4:14 PM

Radar shows a few storms traversing the Alamosa Valley. Most will die later this evening.

# Culebra Peak Bobby's Hill

**14,047 feet** (37° 07' 20" N; 105° 11' 08" W)
**Bivy** August 31–September 1

**Meteorology** **Chris:** Culebra sits far enough south that extra caution should be used during the monsoon months of July and August. I told Jon to expect the normal development of afternoon thunderstorms. I did not see the monsoon playing a significant role, but the typical afternoon activity ran its course over the peak and patience became a virtue on Culebra. Jon waited for the afternoon storms to fade and made his way to the summit for a restful night. Storms continued out on the eastern plains and made for a stellar light show.

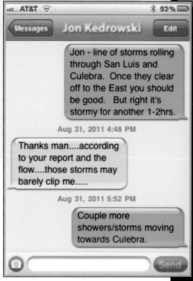

Storms tracked all around Culebra,
but moved out in time for sunset.

## The Harmless Snake

Culebra Peak is privately owned and requires climbers to dig deep into their pockets in order to climb it. I had made special arrangements with ranch owner Bobby Hill and his famous ranch foreman Carlos. I was granted permission to climb Culebra Peak and a few thirteeners, so I proceeded to the trailhead where I found myself all alone at 4:00 p.m. I headed up the trail through tall grasses and sparse trees and waited for my weather window—there were numerous storms in the area. Once again a phone consult with Chris solved the problem. Storms were tracking to the northeast. Chris also confirmed that there was thunderstorm activity over the peak to the east, and a wave of rain with a few lightning strikes about to blow over me coming from the southwest. Once those storms passed over I would be okay to proceed.

After waiting patiently near the timberline, I gained the ridge and cruised up to Culebra's long summit by way of the very long winding ridge. Culebra means "harmless snake" in Spanish, and this description of the peak is fitting. There are no trails in the tundra along Culebra's gentle ridge en route to the summit. Culebra is perhaps the most environmentally pristine four-teener in all of Colorado, because climbing is limited by the Cielo Vista Ranch's $100 fee and the limited number of weekends in the summer that groups are allowed access to the trailhead. While many people object to this management practice of a Colorado Fourteener, my research verifies the pristine nature of the peak, and the validity of the ranch's management of it. While there are very small social trails on a few parts of the high ridges, most hikers disperse while climbing the peak and help to keep the impact to a minimum.

## Thrust-Faulted Summit

Dark hornblende gneiss and layered biotite dominate the summit, placed there by uplifted pegmatite and underlying 1.7-billion-year-old granite. I took advantage of the six-foot Paleozoic rock wind wall built on the summit to set up my tent in strong westerly winds that evening.

Top: Sunset. Above: Sunrise lenticulars.

# Little Bear
# Peak Redemption

**14,037 feet** (37° 34' 0" N; 105° 29' 50" W)
**Bivy** September 2–3

# Nothing Little about Little Bear

Third time is a charm. Little Bear Peak protected its summit from us on two occasions using stormy weather and a ravenous black bear. This third attempt to sleep on its tiny summit was not easy but we threaded the needle. Chris met me at the base of Blanca Massif on a clear Friday afternoon and we pushed toward Lake Como on a mission. His .357 Magnum made his pack a bit heavier, but also showed that we weren't messing around, Little Bears or not. Summer was fading and this peak needed to be checked off the list.

We climbed from the lower parking area on Como Road at 8,000 feet to the summit of Little Bear in four hours flat. I only remember stopping one time en route to wait out a lingering storm. Chris pulled up radar and we watched the clouds swirl.

**Meteorology Chris:** The monsoon hits the Sangre de Cristos hard each year. Why? Because monsoon moisture races in from the south and flows north. This was Jon's third attempt to sleep on Little Bear's summit as violent thunderstorms blanketed the peak on previous occasions. We waited out a thirty-minute storm before proceeding on this attempt. I checked radar numerous times and saw a weather window toward sunset. Jon made a mad dash for the summit while I kept an eye to the sky and radar. The remaining storms either died or moved around Little Bear—it was our lucky night.

Opposite: Sunset looking south. Left: Little Bear from Lake Como. Above: A calm and colorful morning.

Sunrise.

## Cliffside Accommodations

"It's time to go up, Jon," Chris said. We were both huddled behind a giant missile-shaped rock being pelted by small hail and rain. I trusted Chris's weather analysis and we began our ascent toward the Notch on the west ridge in rain that continued to pour. The conditions were terrible still, yet Chris followed. Once on the west ridge, Chris told me to continue on while he re-checked radar, so I put my body into an even higher gear. Chris followed ten minutes later with the "good-to-go" signal, waving his right arm at me like he was hurling a pitch toward home plate.

As the storms pushed east, we were treated with a colorful evening to the north and south of the summit as we headed up the Hourglass of dark-green gabbro. The steep Class 4 Hourglass pitch was drying off in the evening sun and I let off a jubilant yodel as I reached the summit with thirty minutes to spare. I moved some of the angular post-Laramide granite blocks around on the tiny slab of summit and set up the tent, just as Chris arrived in time to help me celebrate with some dramatic sunset shots. Little Bear had finally let us stay the night.

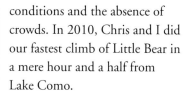

## Summer Conditions

There was a reason Chris decided to carry his gun on Little Bear. A week prior to this final attempt to camp on the summit, I had returned to my truck at the Lake Como trailhead, after being chased off of Little Bear by a storm, only to find a bear had broken the passenger side window and just dove in! There were paw prints all over the interior, on the hood, and even on the roof. The bear took a nice bite out of my cooler, and I found a four-pound container of peanut butter pretzels strewn all over the interior. An entire six-pound bag of whey protein was nowhere to be found! But why didn't the bear eat any of the sausage and elk jerky that was left untouched in my cooler? The bear left plenty of drool on my seats and a trail of gummy bears leading into the woods.

## Winter Conditions

There is no substitute for experience on Colorado's Fourteeners. Between the two of us, we'd climbed Little Bear over ten times. To commemorate one of our memorable snow climbs of the peak, Chris's father David created an acrylic painting of our Little Bear speed ascent in 2010. While many people choose to climb Colorado's Fourteeners in the summer, climbing Little Bear Peak in winter conditions can actually be safer due to the lack of rockfall in snowier conditions and the absence of crowds. In 2010, Chris and I did our fastest climb of Little Bear in a mere hour and a half from Lake Como.

The same experience and knowledge applies to sleeping on the top of any Colorado Fourteener peak. I chose to camp on some of the easier and less technical fourteener summits first, and then do some of the more difficult peaks midway through the project after I had my routines and gear systems planned out to perfection. I also chose to do a difficult summit during the start of a long stretch of peaks so that fatigue could never factor into my ability to succeed, stay on a summit, and descend safely.

Above: Bear break-in.
Right: 2010 winter ascent.

16 x 20 acrylic painting by David Tomer.

# Crestone Peak Conglomerate Cobbles

**14,294 feet** (37° 57' 00" N; 105° 35' 07" W)
**Bivy** September 12–13

Above: Sunset.
Right: Morning—Crestone Peak's flat summit block with
Kit Carson Mountain behind and to the right.

## A Rugged Approach for Three Peaks in Three Nights

Crestone Needle is seen first when tackling the Crestones together from the Cottonwood drainage.

Crestone Peak and Crestone Needle stand in the northern Sangre de Cristo range as two peaks with moderately technical challenge. They were the final set of peaks I had to venture onto for a multi-day backpack in order to complete them. At 3:30 p.m., I arrived at the Cottonwood trailhead, the western and more rugged alternative to the South Colony Basin on the east side. South Colony is a popular trailhead—it's where the majority of climbers begin their assault on the Crestones. I knew I had to move fast and efficiently up the steep trails and peaks, so I packed only enough food for three days, while knowing from Chris that the first major cold front of the season was inbound. My strategy was to get all of my food up near Cottonwood Lake, hang a cache of gear and food in the trees by 6:00 p.m. or so, and then ascend the south face of Crestone Peak, making the summit to spend the night up there by 7:00 p.m., in time for sunset photos.

Cottonwood Basin is rugged, with a narrow trail leading onto boilerplate slabs and through dark evergreen forests. By 5:30 p.m. I was cruising up into an idyllic meadow with a waterfall and approaching timberline. The harsh nature of approaching Crestone Peak is surely why it was the final

Sunrise on one of the more interesting fourteener perches. Winds stayed calm.

**Meteorology Chris:** I remember thinking, *Wow, it might get pretty dicey up there* when Jon called me with his itinerary to camp on the Crestones and Humboldt on consecutive nights. We were approaching what I consider the "fall transition" above tree line in Colorado. You can only plan on the fourteeners to be snow free during July and part of August. In most years, late August and early September usher in a distinct lowering of the snow level on all the fourteeners. I told Jon that he would be just fine on Crestone Peak, but that a significant cold front was headed for the Sangres the very next day. This cold front would bring lightning initially, then snow for his trip up Crestone Needle.

Colorado Fourteener to be scaled as a first ascent by a party consisting of Albert Ellingwood and Eleanor Davis in 1916. Soon I met the Cottonwood Lake trail and a climber's trail leading to the south face of Crestone Peak. I stuck to my plan: I did efficient triaging of some gear that I retrieved the following morning. I left my small laptop, stove, extra food, fuel canister, and a book hanging in a tree near Cottonwood Lake, then I was off to the summit to catch the sunset.

## Paleozoic Sedimentary Thrusted Summit

Skies continued to clear as I approached the steepest part of the climb at 13,000 feet along the flanks of Crestone's north face, also known as the "Red Notch Couloir." Climbing the Class 3 conglomerate rock was quite fun, and I was on the summit in time for sunset. The summit of Crestone is a series of conglomerate summit slabs, raised up to various angles by a series of faults along the crest of the range that broke as the massive block of the range was uplifted in the Laramide Orogeny. To my delight, there was one block that was flat enough and large enough to fit my tent, right at the 14,294-foot summit register!

Once the tent was up, I got some more summit shots and was off to a nice comfortable sleep on the summit block. The full moon came up and there was no wind at all.

I woke in the morning to a spectacular sunrise and also hatched a plan to stay the night on Crestone Needle's summit the next night.

# Crestone Needle

## Echoing Yodels

**14,197 feet** (37° 57' 53" N; 105° 34' 36" W)
**Bivy** September 13–14

Sunrise.

**Meteorology  Chris:**The first Winter Weather Advisories of the season were hoisted for the Sangre de Cristos by the time Jon set up camp on the summit of Crestone Needle. Lightning was minimal during the onset of the afternoon storm, but soon there was only graupel and snow. We texted, but I knew Jon wanted to conserve his phone battery. Jon's plan was to do the Needle then head over to Humboldt for another summit bivy the next day.

I told Jon to expect clearing overnight, but certainly heavy snow the next day. Eight inches seemed likely in the next twenty-four to thirty-six hours.

## Summer to Fall to Winter in Less than Twelve Hours

After taking some spectacular sunrise photos, I dropped off the south face of Crestone Peak and was back down conglomerate slabs and into the gully leading to my gear cache near Cottonwood Lake. My tent had frost on it from my night on Crestone, so I dried it out in the morning sun while I ate oatmeal and some monster cookie bars.

To successfully sleep on Humboldt Peak the following night, I would have to carry all my gear up Crestone Needle that night. My plan was to descend Crestone Needle the following morning then head over to Humboldt—likely in a snowstorm. Although my pack was loaded with everything I needed, it wasn't too heavy. At 10:30 a.m. I was walking past Cottonwood Lake on my way to Broken Hand Pass. Clouds were already building, and the air was much noticeably colder due to it being mid-September. Before I could reach the pass I was pelted by hailstones. It was overcast, and even though Chris said the weather would be good enough to summit and stable enough to stay up on the Needle for the day, I felt like the day would probably get interesting.

Once on Crestone Needle's southeast ridge, I followed a climber's trail to the start of the southeast gullies. Here, at about 13,100 feet, it began to snow lightly. I said to myself, *As long as I can summit in the next hour and set up before it snows heavily, I will be able to get this peak in.*

I didn't see a soul on Crestone Peak the day before, and the same was true of the Needle. Once you get into mid-September, the summer fourteener climbers have retired for the season. I thoroughly enjoyed the gullies of Class 3 and 4 conglomerate knobs as I got into a good rhythm with no worries of other climbers knocking rocks down on me. The flurries continued and I kept a good pace. I wore a stocking cap, but was still in shorts and a short-sleeve shirt because I was generating lots of heat climbing up. I kind of felt like Stallone in *Cliffhanger* on a few moves near the summit with the snow falling before the angle eased and I could go no higher. My watch read high noon. Even with a heavy pack and extra food, I made Crestone Needle look easy. This was my fifth summit of the Needle with my others coming in 1999, 2002, 2005, and 2010. I sounded off an echoing yodel that bounced into the valleys in all directions … it felt great!

## Giant Thrust Fault-block Range

With snow getting heavier and fog engulfing the peaks all around, I set to work on Crestone Needle's accommodating summit. Upper Paleozoic sedimentary rocks, including red sandstone, conglomerate, and shale uplifted in a large fault block. To the west of the range lies the San Luis Valley, and there is a lack of foothills for the mountain range, indicating that it was uplifted in a relatively short geologic time frame. Faults within the range have been inclined, and the layers of rock on Crestone Needle can be clearly observed as a prime example. Just below the true summit of conglomerate, I found a small area I could easily fit my tent. The location also acted somewhat as a natural windbreak. By the time I set up, ate lunch and shot a few pictures, it was approaching 1:00 p.m. Skies were overcast and the snow flurries continued to come down, reminding me that summer was just about over in Colorado, especially at this elevation.

With a look around the summit and the surrounding area, I could see Humboldt Peak to the northeast, Crestone Peak to the west, Kit Carson to the northwest, and the Great Sand Dunes and Blanca Massif to the south. At the moment, the overcast and snow flurries tapered off, so I got in my tent and took a nap.

At 3:00 p.m. I was disturbed by loud thunder from the south. I looked to the west and noticed a dark storm system approaching. A few moments later it started to hail. I was forced to stay put, and I was blasted by hail all afternoon.

The storm never really cleared until after sunset. The snow stopped by 7:00 p.m., but the fog hung around until about 7:30. I was finally able to emerge from my tent to salvage some sunset photos. In the morning I awoke to one of the best sunrises of the entire project!

Opposite: Sunrise with Crestone Peak and the San Luis Valley beyond.

# Humboldt Peak Thunder-snow!

**14,064 feet** (37° 58' 34" N; 105° 33' 19" W)
**Bivy** September 14–15

**Meteorology   Chris:** I was concerned about Jon's safety, but I trusted his field judgment without hesitation. We talked again that morning as Jon hiked over to Humboldt from Crestone Needle in the approaching storm. I knew Jon would make the right decision based on his assessment of conditions in the field. I told Jon I didn't see any lightning in the snow on radar, yet there were a few distant strikes heard that afternoon.

The last time I received word from Jon was from the summit of Humboldt via text. I watched radar all night. This was probably one of the most important accomplishments of the entire project. If Jon would've missed this Humboldt bivy, it would've delayed the project to a point of no return—and we both knew it.

Above: Blue skies soon gave way to thickening fog as the winter storm approached.
Right: Peering down the southwest ridge as the storm rolls in.

Waking up to fresh snow.

## Missing Mom's Birthday in the Winter Storm Warning

I needed to take a huge risk, and as long as I could escape the Sangres alive, it would be a huge rewarding payoff. A dying phone battery, knowledge of a winter storm moving in that day from Chris, and running short on food, I decided to roll the dice. It started snowing that morning on my ascent of Humboldt when I left the Upper South Colony Lake at 11:00 a.m., and it only stopped briefly around one o'clock, just enough time to put up my tent!

The next four to five hours would be critical. How bad would the storm get? Would there be any lightning? If I could just somehow manage to get through the afternoon, I would have no problem staying the night on the peak, even in a blizzard.

At 1:20 p.m. I was sitting in my tent about to unpack all my gear when I heard a series of loud booms coming from the southwest. "Great!" I shouted, "Thundersnow!" I was really worried now. I immediately took out my phone and tried to call Chris. The phone wouldn't dial out, and my battery was almost dead. I managed to send a few text messages.

To Chris at 1:27 p.m.: "On the summit of Humboldt, just got the tent set up and ready to ride out the winter storm … just heard a loud boom to the southwest, can't see anything, and can't even tell where the flow of the storms is coming from."

The boom made me really nervous … would there be more? It appeared that all the winds were coming from the east or even northeast, as the winter storm was probably dropping in from the north, but it was hard to tell in thick pea-soup fog.

To Chris at 1:29 p.m. "Really worried man, can't see anything … should I stay put or bail and come back up? What do you see on radar?"

Then my phone went dead. I was also about to send my Mom a quick text on her birthday, but to no avail. It was up to me and my instincts now. Another loud boom, but this time closer. That's it! I'll leave the tent and go down. I'll just have to come back up later if I can! I grabbed my backpack that I had yet to unpack, and started to hightail it off Humboldt as fast as I could!

## Red Sandstone Whiteout

I should've heeded the warnings of the day before. Chris had told me that I should probably get out of there after Crestone Needle, but I was committed. I didn't want to have to return to that group of peaks. The lightning eventually subsided and I returned to the summit after retreating underneath a ledge at 13,500 feet on the southwest ridge for an hour or so. Humboldt Peak is primarily red sandstone and red shale, but with all that fresh snow it was hard to tell what types of rocks existed. I had my tent securely anchored behind a large rock shelter before the snow started to stick. When I returned at 3:00 p.m., it was buried in a fresh blanket of powder.

I spent the afternoon reading, writing, eating dinner, and brushing off the tent from the inside. Six inches of fresh snow fell by the time the sun went down around 7:15 p.m. The skies never cleared, but there was a brief lull in the snow around this time, which allowed me to get outside for a few photos. No spectacular views of the Crestones on this summit bivy. Once darkness fell, the winds raged out of the southwest and fortunately, the rock shelter I was set up in blocked most of the wind. Summer was definitely over, and for today, the seasons on Humboldt Peak forgot about autumn altogether above 14,000 feet. Once darkness

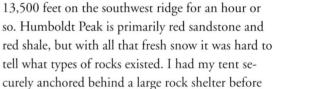

Humboldt from the south the morning before the winter storm hit.

fell, it got really cold as the skies tried to clear. I fell asleep sometime after 9:00 p.m. and only woke up a few times to the sound of the wind and light snow pelting the tent.

In the morning, I packed up in fog and descended into the South Colony Lakes Basin as fast as I could in the fresh powder. Getting back over Broken Hand Pass and down to the Cottonwood Basin and the trailhead was difficult, but I gave it everything I had and made it safely out of there by mid-day.

Opposite: While on Challenger's high northwest ridge, the Great Sand Dunes and the Blanca Massif are seen to the south.

# Challenger Point Ad Astra Per Aspera

**14,081 feet** (37° 58' 49" N; 105° 36' 24" W)
**Bivy** September 16–17

Left: Challenger Point, a mere sub-summit of Kit Carson, but an important landmark.

## To the Stars through Adversity

Located to the northwest of the Kit Carson fourteener is Challenger Point, formerly referred to by many unofficially as Johnny Carson point. The sub-summit was re-named through the proposal of Colorado Springs resident Dennis Williams in memory of the seven astronauts who perished when the Space Shuttle Challenger disintegrated shortly after liftoff in January 1986. The USGS Board of Geographic Names approved the application in 1987.

Since the summit of Challenger is not an official fourteener, I opted to only nap on it and spend the night on the summit of Kit Carson instead. En route to Kit Carson's summit, I still had to pass over Challenger's summit twice. Here are the reasons Challenger is still disputed as an unofficial fourteener:

1. Kit Carson is the highest point, at 14,165 feet, of the entire Kit Carson Mountain, which includes Challenger Point to the west and Columbia Point to the east; both of which are sub-summits of the Kit Carson Massif.
2. Challenger is not named Challenger Mountain, it is named Challenger Point. It is merely a point on the ridge leading to Kit Carson Peak.
3. Some geographic explanations state that if there is a 300-foot drop in the saddle between two peaks, then the second highest point is official. However, many people have stated that Challenger is 301 feet above the saddle. Closer assessment of this through USGS topo maps and newer GPS satellite data actually shows that the saddle rises to 13,783 feet, making the point only 298 feet higher than the saddle, therefore unofficial.
4. It is less than a quarter mile (.23 miles to be exact) from Challenger Point to the summit of Kit Carson in a straight line. USGS surveys state that mountains must be more than a quarter mile apart to be considered separate mountains. Therefore Challenger is not official.

**Meteorology  Chris:** The fall to winter transition season was in full-swing above tree line. Snow and wind continued on both Challenger and Kit Carson. Jon had just dried his gear out from the Crestones and Humboldt. He called me from the town of Crestone before his ascent of Challenger and Kit Carson. I told him the primary storm from Humboldt had cleared, but as is the case in Colorado, the effects of snow and cold almost always linger above tree line for an extra day.

Jon hiked to Willow Lake in sunshine, but the snow and wind began above the lake. It looked brutal.

Opposite: The north face drops 3,000 feet directly from the summit to the right of the tent, with fog blocking all views.

# Kit Carson Mountain

## Yet Another Blizzard

**14,165 feet** (37° 58' 47" N; 105° 36' 09" W)
**Bivy** September 16–17

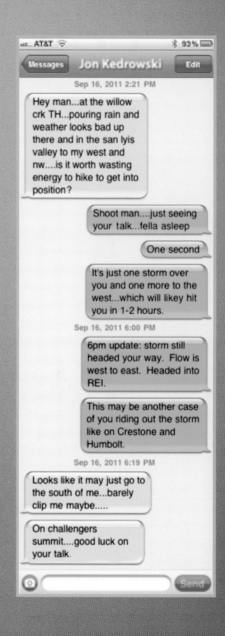

Messages — Jon Kedrowski — Edit

Sep 16, 2011 2:21 PM

Hey man...at the willow crk TH...pouring rain and weather looks bad up there and in the san lyis valley to my west and nw....is it worth wasting energy to hike to get into position?

Shoot man....just seeing your talk...fella asleep

One second

It's just one storm over you and one more to the west...which will likey hit you in 1-2 hours.

Sep 16, 2011 6:00 PM

6pm update: storm still headed your way. Flow is west to east. Headed into REI.

This may be another case of you riding out the storm like on Crestone and Humbolt.

Sep 16, 2011 6:19 PM

Looks like it may just go to the south of me...barely clip me maybe.....

On challengers summit....good luck on your talk.

"Never bivouac." —Gerry Roach

## Ringing in Number 50 Blizzard-Style

This was my last tough technical peak of the project (Class 3). I decided to go for it regardless of the weather and storm chances because the remaining eight peaks would all be relatively easy walk-ups in the Sawatch Range. Heading up the Willow Creek Trail to Willow Lake is a treat—huge conglomerate and granite rock slabs, waterfalls galore, and once again rain! I left my truck at the trailhead at 8,900 feet at 3:00 p.m. in light rain and saw another storm in the San Luis Valley that was coming toward me. Chris indicated that my summit window would be from about 6:00 to 7:00 p.m., then snow would likely move in.

At 6:15 p.m. I was on Challenger Point and the storm was coming. I had cell phone service there and sent some cool pictures to Chris, who was about to give a presentation about our project and mountain meteorology to a group of people at REI-Boulder. They couldn't believe I was up there in a blizzard. Luckily, the only thunder I heard was far south, and there were only a few distant lightning strikes. Most of the storms looked like they were passing south over the Great Sand Dunes.

Normally I wouldn't have pushed to the limit, but at this point in the project I was very confident of my abilities. I forged ahead in heavy snowfall. As I crossed Kit Carson Avenue, there was almost a foot of snow on that ledge. Kit Carson Avenue is not for the faint of heart even in dry weather. It's narrow and is flanked by a sheer drop-off.

Fortunately, I knew exactly where to up-climb the southeast face of the peak. I ascended to the summit in a whiteout, making it by 7:00 p.m., just before the sun went down. Oh, but what sun? You couldn't see anything! The picture quality was marginal at best that evening.

## Conglomerate Joints and Layered Bedding

Red conglomerate dominates the upper reaches of Kit Carson Peak—it is extremely jagged on all sides. Fortunately, the orientation of the conglomerate joints and rock layering creates a weakness that forms a ledge known as "Kit Carson Avenue." This five- to ten-foot wide ledge allows passage around sheer cliffs to find the path of least resistance to the summit. The jagged "Y-shaped" summit ridge is broken by nearly vertical northeast trending joints and steeply cut couloirs. There was a small flat spot directly on the summit where I placed my tent. I knew from past experience that the north face of the peak drops off immediately, so I took special care not to venture too far from the tent. The fog stayed thick all evening, and the snow was on-and-off all night. In the morning I packed up in light snow, and let my instincts take over to help me descend in foggy conditions. Once I dropped below Kit Carson summit, across the Avenue and back across Challenger Point, fog finally cleared and I returned to autumn on the way down to Willow Lake and the trailhead in the San Luis Valley. I had just completed camping on the summit of every fourteener peak in the Sangre de Cristo Range!

Kit Carson Avenue in white-out conditions.

**Meteorology** **Chris:** Jon texted me updates from Challenger while climbing to Kit Carson, which included wind and snow. I knew it was brutal up there and to top it off, another cold front was rolling south that night loaded with snow.

I was pulling double-duty the night Jon ascended Kit Carson. I was providing forecasts to Jon while simultaneously giving a mountain meteorology presentation at REI-Boulder. Talk about irony! Jon texted me a photo during my presentation from the summit of Kit Carson—it was a total whiteout. I texted Jon and told him I didn't see any lightning very close on radar. I shared all this with my audience that night and I was stunned by the looks that came from those seated in front of me.

Messages — Jon Kedrowski — Edit

I hope that thing clips me...snowing now.....

Hey guys! Going up #50...enjoy the talk by tomer!

Damn!!!!!!!

Sep 16, 2011 6:36 PM

Sep 16, 2011 6:56 PM

On the summit....call me during a good time in your talk and put me on speaker! We can do a live chat!

Sep 16, 2011 8:32 PM

Storm moving away from you!!! Should be good!

Sep 16, 2011 9:07 PM

Hey man...phone stopped getting service...wierd!

915...still snowing,! Hhow was your talk.?

Excellent!!

Send

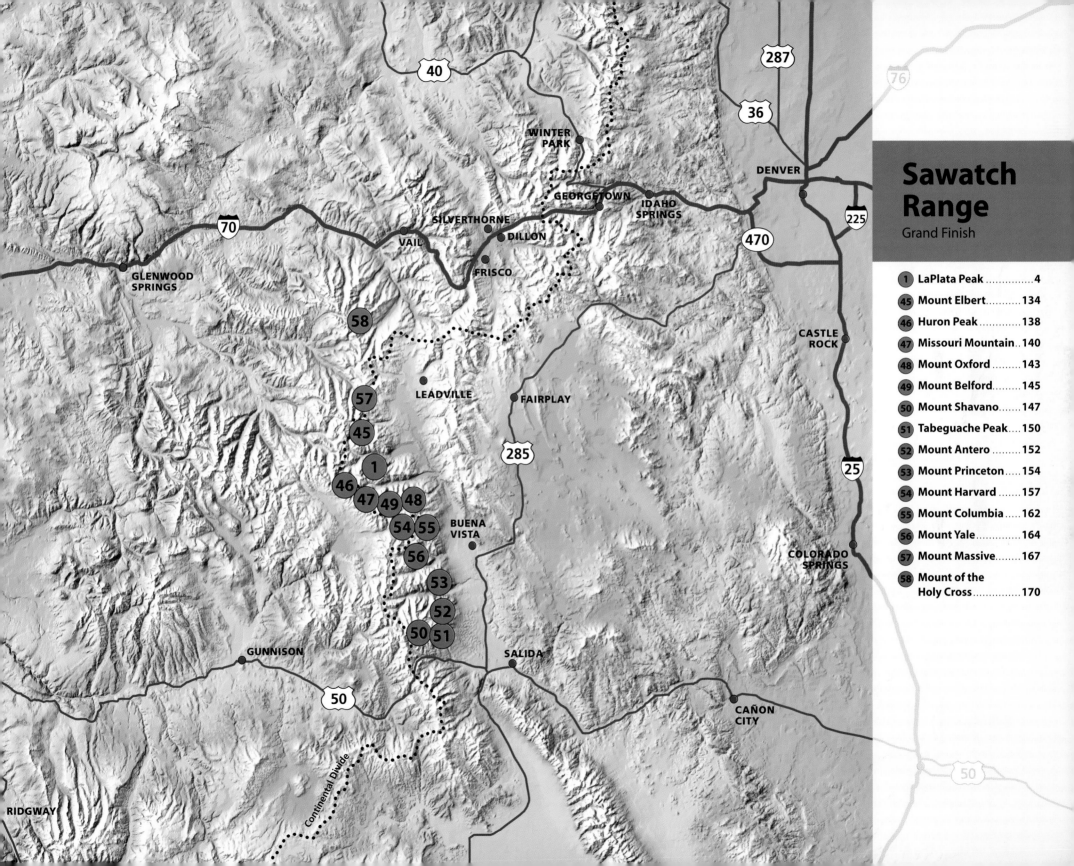

# Sawatch Range

Grand Finish

# Mount Elbert

## Rooftop of Colorado

**14,440 feet** (39° 07' 04" N; 106° 26' 43" W)
**Bivy** August 13–14

Opposite: Mount Elbert from the north.

Right: Sunset.

**Meteorology  Chris:** Mount Elbert anchors the Sawatch Range directly downwind from the Elk Mountains. All mountain ranges force the development of afternoon thunderstorms in the summer months, but Elbert can receive a double dose. Storms blowing off the Elks can hit Elbert after the initial storms have moved east. You can get hit with one storm at 11:00 a.m., then with a second wave of storms later that afternoon. On this occasion a line of late-day storms missed Elbert to the east, setting the stage for a beautiful night.

## A Highpointer's Heaven

I've felt very blessed and lucky to have done so many first-time events with this project. To have spent Wednesday night on Mount Rainier, Washington's highest peak, and then follow that up by spending the night on Colorado's highest peak by Saturday night is probably something that had not been done before in such a short time frame. Add this accomplishment to some of Elbert's more historical firsts, ranging from the first ascent by H.W. Struckle of the Hayden Survey in the 1874, to when the Colorado Avalanche won the Stanley Cup in 2001. Mark Waggoner, an Avs front office executive, carried the cup to the summit in a special backpack. Elbert was named in 1873 for Colorado's territorial governor at the time, Samuel Hitt Elbert.

I had exceptional weather as I hiked up the Colorado Trail/Continental Divide trail from the North Elbert trailhead on Saturday evening. For Colorado's highest, I decided to get out my old blue tent after an eight-peak absence. Mount Elbert is normally climbed in two main ways: via the South Elbert trailhead, or the North Elbert/Halfmoon trailhead, which I chose that evening.

## Highest Camp of All

I climbed quickly from 5:15 to 7:30 p.m. and reached the summit in time to set up on the flat summit ridge. The top of Mount Elbert sees thousands of hikers every summer, and the hundred-yard long summit ridge is flat, with plenty of places to put up a tent among the rounded rocks of biotite gneiss, schist, and migmatite. The northwest to southeast trends in the gneiss and schist are seen near the summit, and are very inclined to almost vertical along the steep side of the ridge. Elbert's high summit was thrust upward and cut by some white dikes of granite and porphyry dating nearly 40 million years old. Some of the oldest rocks near the base of the mountain are almost 2 billion years old.

The next morning I awoke to overcast skies, but the sun found a way to poke through and provide a stellar sunrise. I waited on the summit until mid-morning and greeted some friends that hiked up with Chris before descending, as an oncoming storm front approached from the Elk Mountains. It was bittersweet to know I wouldn't have to camp quite this high again.

Above: Thunderheads building to the east.

Right: Sunrise, summer temperature 35 degrees.

Chilly morning temperatures below zero.

## Birthplace of a Dream

I had a long history of climbing Elbert—multiple climbs and ski descents, moonlight summits in the dark, and training for other peaks by camping on its summit. I grew up less than an hour from Elbert, and took advantage of all the high-altitude training opportunities to climb the multiple routes leading to the summit. In fact, this peak has always been significant to me, and in 2009, while Chris and I camped on the summit before I headed off to Mount McKinley, it was the unofficial birthplace of this crazy idea to camp on the summit of every Colorado Fourteener.

## Highest Dreamers in Colorado

Chris: It was a cold, windy night at 14,440 feet. After all, we were sleeping on the rooftop of Colorado in the winter. Winds gusted to 50 mph that night, snapping one of our tent poles. Overnight temperatures dipped to five below zero. A perfect night for dreaming big.

# Huron Peak
## Mountains in All Directions

**14,003 feet** (38° 56' 44" N; 106° 26' 17" W)
**Bivy** August 15–16

## Powerful Memories

I hadn't set foot on Huron since 2005—and almost exactly six years to the day. On August 14, 2005, it was a day of celebration. Huron is one of Colorado's most isolated and scenic fourteeners. It is deep in the heart of the Sawatch Range, and there are mountains as far as the eye can see. You can also see at least one peak from each of the five other Colorado 14er mountain ranges, and you can see at least forty-five Colorado 14ers on a clear day. Yes, the peak has always been a special one. In 2005, I was celebrating the final fourteener to be climbed that summer, when I was able to climb all fifty-eight Colorado Fourteeners in a span of forty-two days. My parents, Bob and Barb, my older brother Jared, younger sister Krista, their significant others, and my cousin were all there. It was a great day.

Today I was ready to make new memories. Upon reaching the South Winfield trailhead, I tossed a few slices of pizza in my backpack and was off and up the trail rather quickly. There was a storm brewing to the south toward the 13ers known as the Three Apostles. I was going to call to get an update from Chris, but there was no cell service so I pushed on. Throughout the hike up through the woods, the trail switches back and then emerges at the base of Huron's northwest and west faces. The sun was really warm and I filled up my water bottle from a stream at 13,000 feet.

By 6:00 p.m. I was cruising! Up on the northwest ridge I thought I would need a jacket as the wind picked up, but I refused to stop. At 7:00 p.m. the winds died down and I arrived on the tiny and rocky summit.

## Central Sawatch Basement Granite

The tent was set up well before sunset on 1.7-billion-year-old granite known as the Twin Lakes Batholith. The coarse-grained and light grey–layered granite was relatively easy to stack into blocks to anchor my tent and produce a small windbreak, although winds were calm all night. I made a few phone calls to friends and family on the summit, and by 10:00 p.m. found myself dozing off with a full moon rising. It was a gorgeous night on a gorgeous fourteener.

**Meteorology** The storms continued to be a nuisance each and every day in the Sawatch Range as August wore on. I was always concerned that I'd get nailed by a constant monsoon flow from the southwest, so I never let my guard down. Fortunately the Sawatch peaks were very easy to manage. I had detailed logs of past climbs and knew exactly how fast I could make the summits. I would dash up each peak with just enough time to spare and hoped that storms would miss me. Huron and the Belford group that week appeared to have a drier weather pattern than normal for August, which was good news for me.

Left: Sunset in the middle of the Sawatch, with the Three Apostles to the southwest (right). Above: First light.

# Missouri Mountain

## A Bit of Déjà Vu

**14,067 feet** (38° 56' 51" N; 106° 22' 43" W)
**Bivy** August 16–17

Sunset (both).

## Accurate Forecasts: A Critical Project Tool

I spent the morning descending from Huron with a craving for pancakes. When I made it to the base of Huron, I headed over to the Belford-Oxford-Missouri trailhead. After a huge pancake breakfast at the trailhead, I decided that it was a good idea to head up into the Elkhead Basin below Missouri Mountain to be in prime position to make it up to the summit with my overnight gear by sunset. There wasn't any cell service in the basins, but Chris reported only a 20 percent chance of storms for the week, I trekked up five miles and through about three or four waves of storms from 12:30 to 3:00 p.m., carrying a fairly heavy pack because I had food for three days. The strategy was to pick off Missouri first, then to cross over Belford to Oxford for night two and finish with Belford on night three.

I was sitting at 12,600 feet at the start of the Missouri Mountain trail waiting out a storm until 5:00 p.m. In 2006, I camped on the summit of Missouri, and I recalled a memorable conversation with Chris, who had just started working at FOX31 in Denver. That day marked the start of some incredible teamwork. We started our partnership of utilizing the weather forecasts and radar like we do. In the years since then, I have become accustomed to having Chris keep me updated on thunderstorm movements when I climb. In 2006, I was almost to the northwest ridge of Missouri, and when I crested the ridge, off to the west was a big storm. I had cell service, so I called Chris, who told me that he had his fancy weather center radar pulled up to help me. The storm was heading in a different direction and he assured me that I could go up to the summit. With careful review of the clouds, I agreed with him and went for it. That 2006 summit bivy was an important success.

Fast forward to 2011—it was very similar once I reached the north ridge. I was getting pummeled as I approached the ridge, but then my cell phone beeped with a message from Chris: "A few storms to your southwest, moving east, you should be fine." I immediately got on the phone. Upon cresting the ridge there were some nasty looking clouds to the southwest over Taylor Park Reservoir near Gunnison. The flow appeared to be easterly, just as Chris said. It was great to have Chris and the knowledge to know it was safe to go up. Chris and I chatted a few more minutes in excitement about the weather outlook, then I said goodbye and waltzed south along the long ridge to the summit of Missouri.

Top: Storms moving away as the sun sets. Above: A calm morning.

**Meteorology** Chris: It was déjà vu forecasting the weather for Missouri Mountain. I remember talking to Jon on the phone in 2006, when he slept on the summit as a training exercise before he traveled to climb in Kyrgyzstan. We chatted about one remaining thunderstorm cruising across the horizon as the sun was setting. I pulled up radar, zoomed it in, and identified the direction of movement. I gave it my full analysis, including decay and growth trends. The 2006 forecast was strikingly similar to our conversation five years later during this project! I once again pulled up radar, zoomed it in, and analyzed the remaining storm near Missouri Mountain. Like the 2006 storm, this storm was going to clip Jon's summit camp, but then move off to the east. Jon waited on the ridge a mile to the north until the storm passed, then made the top. Technology played a critical role in the success of this climb and all climbs prior. I would always defer the final judgment to Jon. That's one of our cardinal rules: The final decision belongs to the man in the field.

Greeted by a curious goat in the morning.

# Rugged Rarity

Missouri's triangular summit is a little larger than Huron's, with plenty of room for a tent directly on the summit behind a small rock shelter. Granite dominates here, and there are some light-tan to orange porphyry intrusions. The granite here is slightly older than the granite near Huron. The jagged nature of the peak is a rarity for fourteeners in the Sawatch Range, as Missouri boasts one of the only significant moderately technical routes in all of the Sawatch on its southeast ridge. By 7:00 p.m. I had the tent up, ate a sandwich, and settled in to watch the sunset show. A rainbow was forming in the southeast sky from the passing storms, not to mention the stunning views of the Sawatch Range to the south!

# Mount Oxford

## A Break in the Monsoon

**14,153 feet** (38° 57' 53" N; 106° 20' 20" W)
**Bivy** August 17–18

**Meteorology  Chris:** The days were now becoming routine with a dry spell in the monsoon. Jon's biggest dilemma for the Belford group was not the weather forecast, but rather, what to do with all his free time on the summits—sitting around during long afternoons waiting on the sunsets. Luckily Jon took his laptop on nearly every bivy to record a detailed log.

Right: Sunset looking south. Mount Harvard is seen to the left.

Sunrise on Oxford's expansive summit.

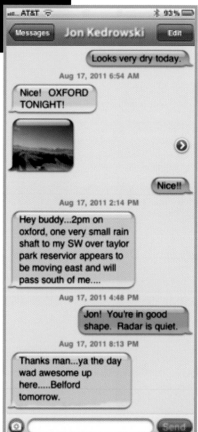

## Passing the Time Above the Timber

I turned my attention to Oxford. Oxford is really nothing more than a long ridge leading to a bump on a ridge above 14,000 feet. From the north ridge of Missouri to Elkhead Pass and up to Belford, there was continuous trail all the way. From the top of Belford I descended to the connecting saddle, then I was on the summit of Oxford by about 11:00 a.m. It was a calm and crisp summer morning.

I met some pretty nice people on Oxford's summit as I passed the time—one pair in particular from New York and Ohio, a father-son duo. I had seen them over on Huron two days prior. The father, Jim, was interested in knowing what my blood oxygen percent saturation was up on the peak, so I put my finger in a little gadget, and he tested me. My resting heart rate up here was 60, which was great for this elevation. My blood oxygen saturation was 91 percent, extremely efficient for this altitude. The experience reminded me of when I was on Aconcagua in early 2010, and I had my oxygen saturation checked out before I could go higher on the mountain. I had just arrived in base camp at 13,600 feet, and yet I tested out to 90 percent, which shocked the docs who were accustomed to seeing 85 percent on someone who had been in base camp for a week! Proper acclimatization is one of the keys to success when you sleep at over 14,000 feet elevation.

## Broken Boulders

It was impossible to put my tent on the direct summit of Oxford because dark-grained granite boulders were crowding the highest point. The summit flats of the peak had plenty of room, however, so I opted for a nice soft grassy spot within a stone's throw of the summit register. I chatted with folks all day, enjoying the warm afternoon sun and lack of storms. I took stock of the remaining peaks and mountain ranges, and went to bed after melting snow for hot drinks after sunset.

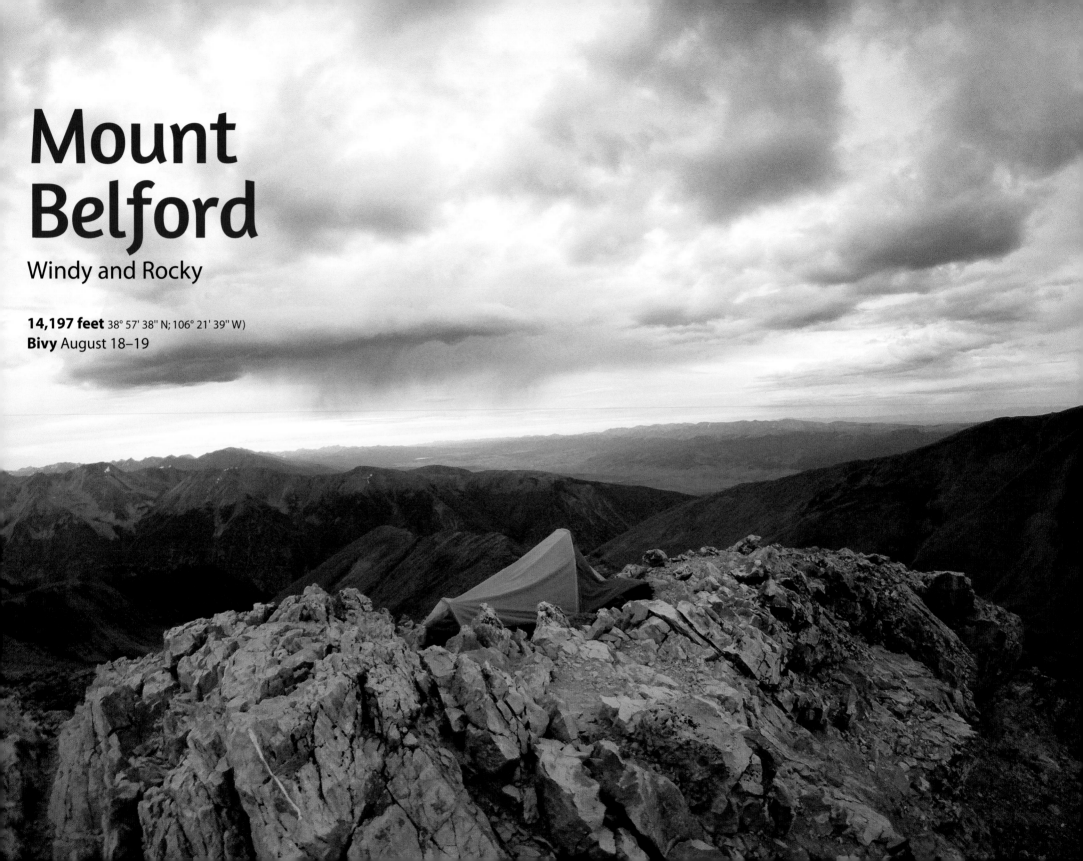

# Mount Belford

## Windy and Rocky

**14,197 feet** 38° 57' 38" N; 106° 21' 39" W)
**Bivy** August 18–19

Previous page:
A clouding evening

Right: Sun rising
over Oxford.

## Fourth Consecutive Night

Belford was my fourth summit bivy in four nights, my fifth fourteener in six nights, and I was still going strong. I woke to a spectacular sunrise on Mount Oxford, ate breakfast, and packed up in high winds. I had an excellent idea for Belford. My plan was to go over to Belford, set up my tent, and then descend in an hour and a half to my vehicle. There I could rest, recover, eat, and wait out storms.

I knew exactly how long it would take me to re-climb the 107 switchbacks on Belford's trail. I ate dinner at 5:00 p.m. at the trailhead, then I quickly returned to the summit with only a few snacks and overnight gear to shoot photos and sleep on the summit, arriving by 7:00 p.m. This was my third time climbing Belford in the past two days!

**Meteorology Chris:** The four-day dry stretch was coming to an end. A big dome of high pressure was starting to weaken and a surge of monsoon moisture was moving north to replace the void. I told Jon that wind speeds were going to pick up for his stay on Mount Belford. These winds are essentially the conveyor belt responsible for transporting moisture into Colorado. The first traces of moisture started to emerge that night on Belford's summit.

## Porphyry and Quartz Outcropping

Earlier in the day, I managed to clear a small spot on one of the rockiest outcroppings I'd seen on all of the fourteeners. Belford's orangeish, white, and tan summit intrusion is composed of porphyry and quartz. While the mountain is primarily granite, it also forms the southern border of the Twin Lakes Batholith. It was a good thing I had anchored the tent and placed a few rocks on the inside earlier that day. Winds were 30 to 40 mph when I returned to the summit that evening under cloudy skies, and I experienced a brief rain shower overnight. The next morning, skies were clearing but you could tell the monsoon was trying to return after a week of dry weather.

Above: Belford's rocky outcropping. Opposite: Sunset.

---

**.... AT&T** ⚡ 93% ▭

**Messages**   **Jon Kedrowski**   **Edit**

Aug 18, 2011 7:11 AM

Morning Jon! Dry day ahead....only a small chance for a PM storm. Fridays forecast isn't looking great :(

Aug 18, 2011 12:33 PM

We'll just get into position below K2 and see what happens.....Belford #37 tonight! Yesterdays weather was awesome on Oxford....today is stellar so far!

Aug 18, 2011 1:00 PM

Excellent job, Jon!

# Mount Shavano

## Angel of Shavano

**14,229 feet** (38° 57' 38" N; 106° 21' 39" W)
**Bivy** September 3–4

A spectacular Shavano September sunset.

## Meteorology

**Chris:** I remember mentioning to Jon how the weather would be changing with the departure of the monsoon. Nights would be getting progressively colder, and the wind speeds would gradually increase as the days passed. Depending on the year, this usually occurs in early September, although 2011 was a year that stands out because the monsoon hung around well into mid-September. As the seasons change, the depth of the atmosphere sitting over Colorado changes—it gets "thinner." Faster winds near the jet stream and the colder air sitting in the higher levels of the atmosphere actually sink down closer to the tops of the fourteeners, therefore the winds become fiercer.

Angel of Shavano.
Below: Closeup.

## Chief Shavano and the Angel

I was driving home to Vail after the stint of peaks in the Sangre de Cristos and passed through Salida and the southern half of the Sawatch Range. The weather looked reasonable on the Sawatch's most southern peak, so I ordered a pizza, loaded up my overnight pack and decided to head up Shavano for the night to get another peak knocked off.

The Ute Indians of the region named Shavano after one of their leaders. Chief Shavano was a sub-chief of the Uncompaghre Ute Indians. He was loyal and friendly toward the white settlers of the upper Arkansas Valley. Chief Shavano played an intricate role in promoting peace between white settlers and the Indians, and was noted for his friendship with Kit Carson, an early Colorado explorer. Despite his help with recovering white captives following the Meeker Massacre of 1879, Shavano and other Utes in the area were deported to Utah in 1881. Shortly thereafter, prospectors in the region noticed the outstretched arms of the intersecting gullies that held snow below Shavano's southeast face, which created the Angel of Shavano. It was said that Shavano used to pilgrimage to the mountain every year to pray for his people. Therefore, in his absence, there was an angel left behind to keep watch over the valley and its inhabitants forever. In most years the angel appears with the spring snowmelt, with two outstretched arms and a small head. Due to recent warming trends, the angel is almost completely melted away by mid-June, and is clearly visible from Salida.

After observing the angel myself en route to the Shavano trailhead, I arrived at the trailhead at 4:00 p.m. and slowly made my way up through aspens and evergreens. When I emerged from the trees heading up the east side of the peak it began to hail. The hail was light and there was no lightning, and upon further consult with Chris at 5:30, he said I could continue to the summit as the weather was clearing off to the west.

## Granite Summit

I made Shavano's rather rocky summit at 6:15 p.m., pretty exhausted, and got all set up. I was fatigued probably because I had recently finished a long stretch of peaks in the Sangre de Cristos, including Little Bear. The light-colored granite of the Mount Princeton Batholith dominates the summit. I stayed on the eastern aspect of the summit and used the large boulders as protection from a light wind out of the west. Once the spectacular sunset showed off its colors, the temperatures dropped into the twenties for the night with no wind.

The start of fall had hit the upper peaks, as I awoke in the morning to some frost on my tent, and a light dusting of snow. Once the morning sunrise show was over, I quickly retreated down the mountain and arrived at the safety of my truck by 8:30 a.m.

# Tabeguache Peak Chief Tab-uh-wash

**14,155 feet** (38° 37' 32" N; 106° 15' 03" W)
**Bivy** September 18–19

**Meteorology** That afternoon on Tabeguache was the first time in months that I could completely let my guard down in regards to afternoon storms. But, anytime you combine clearing skies with a passing cold front and a calm evening, temperatures will drop rapidly overnight so bundle up! It was one of the coldest nights of the entire project—when I awoke that morning, my thermometer showed 8-degrees Fahrenheit!

Above: Sunrise. Right: Sunset.

## Monsoon Over, Indian Summer Arrives

The excitement of this project nearing completion finally sunk in when I approached the summit of Tabeguache. How appropriate for the summer monsoon to finally end, the snow and blizzards to finally subside, and for the colors of Indian summer to show their full splendor deep in the heart of my final mountain range of the Sawatch.

In recent days, the monsoon subsided because cold fronts had approached from the northwest. Skies had cleared, and the air was a bit colder. The evenings had a little bit of a bite to them. In perfect harmony, Indian summer found me spending a spectacular night on a peak in the southern Sawatch named for another Indian chief from the late 1800s: Tabeguache. Long ago, Ute Indian tribes roamed these portions of central Colorado and eastern Utah. They may have even found their way to the summits of these southern Sawatch peaks prior to the Wheeler and Hayden Surveys of the 1870s.

## One of the Coldest Nights of the Project on a Dike of Granite

In order to summit Tabaguache Peak, I had to climb up and over Shavano, again. Even though the Shavano climb was only two weeks prior, this time snows of the past week coated the upper portions and the summits of both Shavano and Tabegauche.

Skies cleared that evening, and in the morning temperatures were in the single digits before the sun came up. Fortunately, winds were light. The summit lies just west of the border of the Mount Princeton Batholith. Rocks on this summit were streaky granite along with grey quartz and pink feldspar crystals. These rectangular contrasting rocks provided excellent tent anchors, and gave the small flat summit an interesting look along with the fresh snow that was dropped in a storm only a couple days earlier. Much like the days of old, I was treated to the howl of coyotes as the sun went down over the basin to the west.

# Mount Antero Colorado Gems

**14,269 feet** (38° 37' 32" N; 106° 15' 03" W)
**Bivy** September 19–20

Sunset.

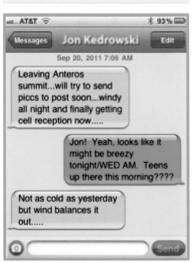

## Second Chief In a Row

With temperatures in the mid-seventies in the Arkansas River Valley, I kept the spirit of the Indian summer true and headed up Antero the next day. The aspens were changing rapidly to gold as I departed my truck near Baldwin Creek. There is a reasonable four-wheel-drive road that climbs all the way up to 13,800 feet on the southwest flank of Antero, and this area is a popular summer motorized recreational area.

I followed the road for parts of the standard route of the western and southern slopes of Antero. Above 13,000 feet it got windy, but the sun was warm. In a mere two hours I made my way across the final south ridge of the peak. Once on the summit, I displayed the return of my vintage blue tent to match the brilliant colors of the sky and the awesome sunset. After the sun went down, the evening winds came rushing through from time to time, and it was the least amount of sleep I have gotten on a peak in over a week.

## A Sea of Aquamarine

Not only is Antero the tenth highest peak in Colorado, named for Uintah Indian Chief Antero, but various gemstones have been known to be found on its slopes. This area is famous for some of the highest concentrations of Aquamarine in the world (a silicate mineral beryl: $Be_3Al_2(SiO_3)_6$). Still a part of the Mount Princeton Batholith, the granite on the summit is very flat, with plenty of soft dirt to place my tent on, including angular light grey, medium-grained granite to anchor the tent from the wind.

# Mount Princeton

## Eye of the Tiger

**14,197 feet** (38° 44' 57" N; 106° 14' 33" W)
**Bivy** September 20–21

Above: Staying behind the rock shelter at sunrise in 50 mph winds.

Right: The setting sun behind a distant shaft of rain and snow.

## Bring on the Collegiate Peaks!

Climbing Mount Princeton for the night was the epitome of "dash and crash" as far as this project was concerned. My adrenaline was pumping, knowing I had less than a week left until the end of the project. Princeton was the sixth peak in seven nights, and the eighth peak in ten nights, so I took advantage of my truck's power and braved the rather easy Mt. Princeton Road. The road ascends from 8,000 feet to nearly 12,000 feet in about six miles, where narrow parking is available. I arrived at the highest parking I could find at about 4:00 p.m., and with nothing but sleeping gear, tent, a couple of sandwiches, water, a candy bar for breakfast, and a peach, I cruised up the east face and ridge of Princeton. I was prancing like a tiger all the way, reaching the summit in a mere hour and a half at an easy pace.

Princeton's east face.

Windy across the southern Sawatch.

...AT&T 🔋 93%

**Messages**  **Jon Kedrowski**  **Edit**

Sep 21, 2011 5:52 AM

Nice and windy up here on Princeton this morning! How's it going for you man?

Jon!! Going ok! Beautiful forecast ahead!!!! Still working out schedule for next were. I give it a 50/50 chance. You're almost DONE Jon!!!

Sep 21, 2011 2:00 PM

Beautiful day here in Denver

Send

**Meteorology**  In the morning, I was careful to stay below the shelter and out of the wind as I packed up the tent. In winds exceeding 50 mph, and temperatures below freezing, frostbite can set in quickly if you aren't careful!

Chris: With the end of the summer monsoon comes the return of wintertime winds. The atmosphere actually shrinks, allowing the faster winds of the jet stream to descend on the 14er summits. When you climb in the fall and winter months, be ready for high winds—take gloves, hats, and even a balaclava. Jon felt the fierce winds of fall on Princeton. In many ways these winds result in down-valley warming. These Chinook winds are advected to lower elevations like Denver, Colorado Springs, and even the banana belt of Chaffee County.

In 1877, the first documented ascent of Princeton was by a Princeton graduate named William Libbey. Henry Gannett of the Wheeler Surveys by sheer coincidence had named the peak Mount Princeton four years prior. In those days there was no road up the peak. Today the 6,500-foot vertical gain from the surrounding valleys is rarely ascended on foot as in those days. Most climbers take advantage of the Mt. Princeton Road in a vehicle at least for part of the ascent.

## Mount Princeton Batholith and the Chalk Cliffs

The triangular summit of Princeton has seen thousands of hikers over the years, and I would bet that many people have already camped on the summit. I took advantage of getting behind a five-foot grey granite wall from the Princeton Batholith. There were plenty of rocks present to keep the tent sheltered and anchored from a second consecutive night of brutal winds. It was probably the windiest night for sustained winds thus far in the project, but you are going to get that type of weather when the fall season arrives.

To the east and southeast of the peak there are chalk cliffs known well by the locals. Hot springs from the subsurface boil up and react with the granite to change the composition of the rock, softening it up to form these chalky cliffs. The Mount Princeton Hot Springs are one of the more famous hot springs in Colorado.

Opposite: Sun setting at 7:30 P.M., storms dying off to the north, or so I thought.

# Mount Harvard

## Zapped Under St. Elmo's Fire

**14,420 feet** (38° 55' 28" N; 106° 19' 15" W)
**Bivy** September 21–22

Sunset.

**Meteorology Chris:** What happened on Harvard that night was my nightmare scenario from the start of the project. After the daily thunderstorms developed and completely died with the sunset, one last rogue storm re-emerged. This storm snuck in while Jon was about to crash in his tent for the night. The tailend of a cold front was diving through the mountains that night. It was a minor front, but oftentimes the mountains enhance even the smallest of weather features.

## One-Point-Twenty-One Jigawatts of Power

Skies were clearing after the sun went down on Colorado's third highest peak. I went through my usual routine of finishing my sunset photos and brushing my teeth. It was nearly the Autumnal equinox and skies were already dark by 7:30 p.m. Satisfied with the clearing skies and calm winds, I sought refuge in the tent to read a book and call friends with good cell phone coverage. By 9:30 p.m. my eyes were heavy and I was ready to call it a night. I reached to turn my phone off and it lit up with an incoming call from a dear friend, who was checking up on me to see how I was holding up.

Ten minutes later our conversation was interrupted by a flash that lit up the tent. A crash of thunder followed soon after. I poked my head out of the tent to see what was going on. A large storm fifty miles to the east had some lightning, but it was apparently drawing the energy and the air from directly over my head on Harvard's summit. "I gotta get off of here!" I shouted. There was another flash and an instant boom, and to my friend on the other end of the line, the phone went dead.

Sunrise the morning after the tent was struck by lightning.

## Nearly Zapped from Existence

There was so much power, so much energy on that summit that sparks were flying. I grabbed my backpack and jacket, slipped my shoes on, and before I could stand up, the entire summit area was buzzing to life and lit up with powerful charges. I didn't even need a flashlight! The two previous strikes were close, but I knew that at any moment the tent and where I was standing was going to get struck. As the energy continued to build, I literally slid down the south aspect of the summit block cradling my backpack. The phone call from my friend may have saved my life because it had kept me awake!

The thunder sounded like a bomb going off. It was like a war up there and diving down off that peak into the rocks was such an adrenaline rush and it all happened so fast! When that buzzing of energy charging the summit came, I knew what to do, yet I couldn't believe that I was able to drop off the summit block in time. When the major bolt shot through the tent, I was fifty feet below the summit and *sprinting* down the trail in a whiteout, yet I still felt the heat of the bolt on my body's left side.

## Mount Harvard Guardian Angels

The entire summit was lit up with charges. I kid you not—I looked out and saw an angel pointing down off the top, showing me where to go to get off that summit block. The way down was brightly lit like an airport runway. I safely made my way down a few thousand feet in pelting hail, which stopped less than an hour later. Suddenly the stars came out, the fresh snow lit up the trail, and I realized I must have lost my headlamp in haste. Hours later when I returned to the tent, I zipped open the tent flap and found my fried headlamp and charred battery remains resting on my sleeping bag. The angel had lit a path for me to find my way down safely.

Right: Storm damage.

**Messages** **Jon Kedrowski** **Edit**

Sep 21, 2011 7:18 PM

Haaarvard.....rocky summit block....!

#54....4 to go...post to fb please...about to get clipped by a snow storm,!

Sep 22, 2011 4:03 AM

That storm last night came outta nowhere! Scariest moment of my entire life......back on harvard since bailing from 930 til midnight......havent slept a wink in 4 hours.......

Sep 22, 2011 4:34 AM

Wow....that is the nightmare scenario I've worried about since June: sleeping and a storm rolls in. Soooooo glad you're ok. Radar is clear now.

## Near-Death Experience

Chris: On both pages are our actual text conversations and the associated radar imagery. The weather was deceptively clear when Jon entered his tent for the night at 7:30 p.m. It was a different story by 9:30 as the storm literally formed directly over the summit on the tail end of a cold front. The electrical charges hit the summit fast, with the hailstorm included. By 10:30 the storm cleared, and Jon climbed back up to the tent to find it was baked pretty good by the resulting lightning strikes. When Jon assessed the damage in the morning with better light, he found he'd escaped with his life, an experience with a guardian angel, and a tent with bolt holes, burnt tent fabric, burnt trail shoes, and melted poles.

cold front

Cold front moving in—conditions just before dark were priming for storm development.

Summit at 7:30 P.M.

# Mount Columbia

## Flawless Fall Evening

**14,073 feet** (38° 54' 14" N; 106° 17' 51" W)
**Bivy** September 22–23

Left and right: Sunset with Yale in the distance.

## Cold and Crisp Confidence to Climb Columbia

Fresh off being nearly sent "Back to the Future" by a bolt of lightning on Harvard, I went back up into Horn Fork Basin and to the summit of Columbia for a night on top. Many people have asked me how it felt to go back up a summit on the very next night after what happened to me on Harvard. My response is always the same, and it is truly a life lesson: Success is measured simply by getting up one more time than you have been knocked down. That's what this project was all about. In life, you are constantly climbing mountains and taking risks in everything you set out to accomplish if the task is worthwhile. I'll admit that I didn't sleep as well on the remaining summits after what transpired on Harvard. I peered out of my tent in clear skies being "on guard" for storms on those last few nights more times than I needed to. But, when it was time to go up the last four summits, I did not hesitate. The finest hours of the project had come, and I wasn't going to fold, I had already made it too far.

It certainly helped that the fall colors were really looking stellar in the basin. Columbia is a very easy climb, up the west slopes and to the south ridge. Calm winds, sunny skies, and a spectacular sunset were the highlights.

**Meteorology** Colorado "bluebird" days are most common during the winter, and the pre-monsoon spring months of May and June. You can also get close to a bluebird day in the post-monsoon season in late September. That evening on Columbia was one of those days, with the exception of high cirrus clouds that made for an outstanding orange sunset.

## Giants of Granite Proportion

There are so many large boulders on Columbia's summit that I set up a modified tent shelter using my tent's rain-fly over a small rock shelter. The boulders are very similar on both Columbia and neighboring Harvard, comprised of 1.7-billion-year-old granite. The darker the granite on these summits, the more biotite present within the vertical streaky structure of the rocks.

Sunrise after a night under the stars.

# Mount Yale Sixth Consecutive Night

**14,196 feet** (38° 50' 39" N; 106° 18' 50" W)
**Bivy** September 23–24

## An Unprecedented Run of Peaks

Mount Yale in the Sawatch Range was a great way to end one of the most spectacular, memorable, and even dangerous stretch of peaks during the entire project. By the time I stood on the summit in warm sunshine Friday evening, I had capped a streak that was one of the greatest in depth of this project: eleven peaks in thirteen nights, six peaks in six nights. In retrospect I had really climbed thirteen peaks in thirteen nights if you included having to go up and over Shavano, and having to climb back up Harvard after the lightning event.

Yale gave me a relaxing night on a peak with brilliant sunset colors, light winds, and relatively warm overnight temperatures. There were a few clouds that night as the sun went down and a minor set of hailstorms that stayed to the south and east over Princeton and Antero, adding to the dramatic backdrop. Once darkness fell, I was still afraid that a thunderstorm might develop right over me, so I waited until I saw stars in the sky before I retired for the night.

Opposite: Sunset.

Above: Harvard in the distance served as a reminder to never let my guard down during the final peaks.

**Meteorology  Chris:** I wasn't worried about Jon while he was on Yale. Due to a week's worth of Indian summer, there was very little fresh snow on the Collegiate Peaks when Jon slept on Yale's summit. Overnight temperatures were touching 10 degrees, but the daytime sun was intense, causing a lot of the snow on those peaks to melt. Winds were calm, while the afternoon storms were small and missing Jon's location.

Yale's shadow (left) with storms over Princeton and Antero (right).

High scattered stratocumulus clouds at sunrise.

## Oldest Rocks in the Sawatch Range

The summit of Yale boasts mixtures of igneous and metamorphic rocks. White plutonic igneous rock is also present. The summit ridge is long and narrow, and among the specimens of granite are also jagged dark boulders of 1.8-billion-year-old gabbro, some of the oldest known rocks in the Sawatch Range. Fortunately for me, the winds were light because there weren't enough blocks to build a suitable windbreak.

In the morning, there was yet another memorable sunrise as I departed the summit and headed back to the trailhead.

# Mount Massive

## A Massive Detour

**14,421 feet** (39° 11' 15" N; 106° 28' 33" W)
**Bivy** September 26–27

Top: Atop Colorado's second highest peak, with Mount Elbert to the south engulfed in a passing evening storm. Above: First light over Lake County.

## Motorcycle Power

The primary access to Mount of the Holy Cross was closed during the summer of 2011. However, I was told I could ride a motorcycle up the Tigiwon Road to access Mount of the Holy Cross, which would've made Mount Massive the final peak. But when I arrived at the start of Tigiwon Road that day, I was stopped by a forest ranger who told me that even motorcycles were not allowed up the road. Sometimes in life you have to expect the unexpected, handle changes with a smile on your face, and take advantage of a new opportunity.

I quickly improvised, and I immediately turned the dirtbike up Highway 24. I rode up and over Battle Mountain Pass, Tennessee Pass, behind Leadville on some dirt roads, and before 4:00 p.m., I was within minutes of the North Halfmoon trailhead. My brother Jared's motorcycle gave me quick and easy access up a dirt road to the trail leading up the east side of Massive.

I locked up the motorcycle around some trees, and by 4:30 p.m. was headed up the peak via the North Halfmoon trail. The east side of Mount

Brilliant sunset with storms in the area.

**Meteorology  Chris:** I remember Jon changing his itinerary at the last minute from Holy Cross to Mount Massive. Either way, I wasn't worried about the weather forecast. The weather pattern had officially shifted to autumn with minimal afternoon cloud and storm development. There was only a small chance of graupel or flurries that night above the timber, and it happened to randomly develop over Mount Elbert to the south. Nights were clearing like clockwork, and overnight low temperatures were routinely around 10 degrees on the summits.

Massive is wild, rugged, and remote. The trailhead is at roughly 10,600 feet, and in a little more than 3.5 miles, I would gain almost 4,000 vertical feet and arrive on the summit of Massive before sunset. But, I had to put the hammer down yet again!

Once leaving the valley, the trail switch-backed up the east slopes of the peak, and the views just got better and better. By 6:20 p.m. I was on the summit ridge. I was keeping tabs on a small set of storms stretching over Mount Elbert and the rest of the Sawatch Range to the south.

## Expansive Real Estate Above 14,000 Feet

All storms appeared to be moving east, and after I set up my tent, I got some dramatic sunset photos. Not only were the fall colors impressive, but the nearby storm added a nice touch of color and danger that kept me on guard the entire evening. Storms that impact hikers on Massive can be devastating, simply because it is a very long way to the safety of tree line. Mount Massive has a total of five summits all over 14,000 feet, and the summit ridge stays above 14,000 feet for more than three miles.

A majority of the summit ridge is granite, comprised of biotite gneiss, migmatite, and schist. The sheer volume and surface area of Massive boasts the highest amount of land area above 14,000 feet in the entire Lower-48. Properly named since 1873, the peak has been petitioned more than once by authorities in Denver to be named Gannett Peak, and even Mount Evans. However, the citizens of Leadville have always protested for the name to be kept the same and for good reason.

# Mount of the Holy Cross

## Fight to the Finish

**14,005 feet** (39° 28' 01" N; 106° 28' 54" W)
**Bivy** September 27–28

Above: Historical view of Holy Cross from Notch Mountain.

Right: Jubilation as the sun sets on the final peak.

**Meteorology   Chris:** The end was near and the weather could not have been better. Jon texted me his itinerary and I was so excited for him and the completion of this project. I was not expecting any thunderstorms or cold fronts. Those moments of Jon hitting the summit will surely be etched in time forever.

Sunrise.

# A Tough Test: A Bushwack and a Classic Finish

Time was running out, but the weather was exceptional, and the moment had finally arrived—I was on my last peak.

When I pulled into the closed gate and parked my truck, the clock read 2:00 p.m. I knew that in order to make it up the entire Tigiwon Road and hike to the summit of Holy Cross before sunset, I would have to put on an incredible performance. Because the closure of Tigiwon Road had basically prevented people from climbing Holy Cross all summer, I was banking on not seeing a soul up there. If something went wrong, there would be nobody to see it, and nobody to turn to. I didn't care, I kind of liked the situation and the solitude. It was just me and the mountain now. The Indian summer day was nice and warm, and the fall colors were beautiful. Nothing else mattered now—it was time to finish this project once and for all!

I was about to enter the finest twenty-four hours of this project. So many forces were stacked against me. I put on my pack and started pedaling up the Tigiwon road on my mountain bike. Soon I decided to ditch the mountain bike and I ventured into the Cross Creek Basin, a route rarely traveled by the climbers of Holy Cross. Call it the "back road" to the summit.

Above: Bike was abandoned in the woods en route to the final bivy. Right: Fall colors entering the Cross Creek drainage.

All packed up and
ready to go home.

For the next two hours, I traversed a gorgeous glacial trough basin full of aspen groves, small ponds, low lying bogs, and a mountain that encouraged me to push on. By 4:30 p.m., the mountain was clearly in view and the only problem was time. Escaping this idyllic basin was going to take a monumental bushwhack! I had to make the summit in time for sunset.

At 5:00 p.m. I found a way to get across Cross Creek, and some serious power and determination pushed me up toward Holy Cross's northeast ridge. There were many times that I thought I'd never gain the ridge, or even get out of the woods, but these were my final two hours and I wouldn't be denied.

At 6:00 p.m. I emerged onto the main Holy Cross Peak trail and passed timberline. Lots of cairns marked the ridge up there, but I don't know why. I could see the summit and knew exactly where I was headed. The summit and the final bivy were waiting for me. The skies were crystal clear, and it was all up to me now—make the summit before sunset and make history, or sit down and be denied. The former was the only choice I would accept.

## Metamorphic Summit for the Ages

I climbed the final summit ridge and came up over some granite, as well as biotite, schist, and migmatite boulders—and then saw the coveted summit. Though I was out of breath, I knew that I'd remember this moment forever. I shot some video as I approached the summit. After a little summit dance, I quickly got the tent up amidst the setting sun, and enjoyed the evening. To do something that has never been done before is really special, yet I didn't quite know how to feel. All I can say is that it was humbling, satisfying, fulfilling, a test of patience, and a huge sigh of relief.

Jon in front of Longs Peak.

# Afterword

So many people were counting on me during this project, and so many more decided to follow along. Thanking you isn't nearly enough, but right now it's the best I can do. This project is also proof that overcoming odds, taking risks, staring death in the face, and never giving up are real values that lead to success. Giving something everything you have and pouring your heart into adversity are all real issues in life that we may all face. I faced these problems mainly with the forces of nature, and with adversity that comes with the dangers that waited to literally snuff the life out of me. Yet I am proof that nothing is impossible; everything can be gained, you just have to go out there and refuse to give in, refuse to surrender. Call on the expertise and motivation of friends to get you up the proverbial mountain of life. Inspire yourself to be great, that's what I did, and I had a lot of fun during the entire journey.

# Colorado Fourteeners 14,000 feet and Mount Rainier 14,411 feet

I've felt truly blessed to have the kind of energy, drive, and passion for the mountains to endure high summits, storms, snow, and high winds. I also enjoyed some great weather toward the end to put many of these summit bivy streaks together. I relied on Chris Tomer's weather expertise to help get me through safely.

Summary of Ascents: Climbed to the summit of all 58 named Colorado Fourteeners and spent the night on the 55 "official" fourteener peaks starting on June 23, 2011, with La Plata Peak in the Sawatch Range, and finishing with Mount of the Holy Cross on the morning of September 28, 2011. Ninety-five days for 55 summit nights, and I climbed 73 peaks to the summit, including a bivy in the summit crater of Mount Rainier in Washington. Here are some notable streaks in the project that included three consecutive overnight bivys or more on several occasions: 1) San Luis, Handies, Uncompaghre, Sunshine, and Redcloud; 2) Eolus, Sunlight and Windom; 3) Mt. Wilson, Wilson Peak, El Diente, and Sneffels; 4) Lincoln, Democrat, Bross, and Quandary; 5) Both Maroon Bells and Pyramid; 6) Grays, Bierstadt, Evans, Torreys, Longs, and Pikes; 6) Crestone Peak, Crestone Needle, and Humboldt; 7) Tabeguache, Antero, Princeton, Harvard, Columbia, and Yale. To the author's knowledge, no single person has ever spent the night on every Colorado Fourteener, and certainly not in one summer season.

But the story doesn't end here. In mid-August 2011, I climbed Mount Rainier, the highest mountain in Washington state. On that trip, after guiding friends to the summit and back down safely on the morning of August 10, I started back up the peak that same afternoon, climbing Mount Rainier twice in one day, and spending the night on the summit of the 14,411-foot volcano that evening.

When I spent the night on that summit, I couldn't help but wonder—What about climbing the highest peaks in other states in the United States, or across the globe? Hmmm..........

Sunset Wednesday, August 10.

Sunrise Thursday, August 11.

# Appendix A: 2011 Chronology–Summer Fourteener Log

## Peaks Climbed and Summit Bivouacs

| Peak Name (Elevation in Feet) | Mountain Range | Dates of Bivouac or Climb (2011) | Route(s) Climbed to Summit (Difficulty–Class) |
|---|---|---|---|
| **1. La Plata** (14,336') | Sawatch | Thu–Fri, June 23–24 | Southwest Ridge (C2) |
| 2. Wetterhorn (14,015') | San Juan | Mon–Tue, June 27–28 | Southeast Ridge (C3) |
| 3. San Luis (14,014') | San Juan | Wed–Thu, June 29–30 | South Ridge (C1) |
| 4. Handies (14,048') | San Juan | Thu–Fri, June 30–July 1 | West Slopes (C2) |
| 5. Uncompahgre (14,309') | San Juan | Fri–Sat, July 1–2 | East Slopes (C2) |
| 6a. Sunshine (14,001')** | San Juan | Sat, July 2 | East Ridge (C2) |
| 7. Redcloud (14,034') OB | San Juan | Sat–Sun, July 2–3 | Sunshine /South Ridge (C2) |
| 6b. Sunshine (14,001') | San Juan | Sun–Mon, July 3–4 | Redcloud/ North Ridge (C2) |
| 8. Eolus (14,083') | San Juan | Thu–Fri, July 7–8 | Upper Northeast Ridge (C4) |
| 9. North Eolus (14,039') X | San Juan | Fri, July 8 | South Ridge (C2+) |
| 10. Sunlight (14,059') OB | San Juan | Fri–Sat, July 8–9 | South Slopes (C4) |
| 11. Windom (14,082') OB | San Juan | Sat–Sun, July 9–10 | West Ridge (C2+) |
| 12. Mount Wilson (14,246') | San Juan | Wed–Thu, July 13–14 | North Face via Navajo (C4) |
| 13. Wilson Peak (14,017') | San Juan | Thu–Fri, July 14–15 | West Ridge (C3) |
| 14. El Diente (14,159') OB | San Juan | Fri– Sat, July 15–16 | Kilpacker South Face (C3) |
| **15. Sneffels** (14,150'), OB | San Juan | Sat–Sun, July 16–17 | East Slopes (C2+) |
| 16. Cameron (14,238') X | Tenmile/Mosquito | Tue, July 19 | West Ridge (C2) |
| 17. Lincoln (14,286') | Tenmile/Mosquito | Tue–Wed, July 19–20 | Cameron/West Ridge (C2) |
| 18. Democrat (14,148') | Tenmile/Mosquito | Wed–Thu, July 20–21 | East Ridge (C2) |
| 19. Bross (14,172') | Tenmile/Mosquito | Thu–Fri, July 21–22 | West Slopes (C2) |
| **20. Quandary** (14,265') | Tenmile/Mosquito | Fri–Sat, July 22–23 | East Ridge (C1) |
| 21. Sherman (14,036') | Tenmile/Mosquito | Sun–Mon, July 24–25 | Iowa Gulch, West Slopes (C2) |
| 22a. Castle (14,265') | Elk | Mon–Tue, July 25–26 | Northwest Ridge (C2+) |
| 23. Conundrum (14,060') X | Elk | Tue, July 26 | Southwest Ridge (C2+) |
| 22b. Castle (14,265') | Elk | Tue, July 26 | Gear Retrieval (C2+) |
| **24. Maroon Peak** (14,156') | Elk | Wed–Thu, July 27–28 | South Ridge (C3) |
| **25. North Maroon** (14,014') | Elk | Thu–Fri, July 28–29 | Bells Traverse S. to N. (C4) |
| 26. Pyramid (14,018') | Elk | Fri–Sat, July 29–30 | Northeast Ridge (C4) |
| 45a. Capitol (14,130') *** | Elk | Sat, July 30 | Knife Edge–NE. Ridge (C4) |
| 27. Bierstadt (14,060') | Front | Sun–Mon, July 31–Aug 1 | West Slopes (C2) |
| 28. Grays (14,270') | Front | Mon–Tue, Aug 1–2 | North Slopes (C1) |
| 30a. Torreys (14,267')*** | Front | Tue–Wed, Aug 2–3 | South Slopes/Ridge (C2) |
| 29. Evans (14,264') | Front | Wed–Thu, Aug 3–4 | Mount Evans Rd. /S. Trail (C1) |
| 30b. Torreys (14,267') | Front | Thu–Fri, Aug 4–5 | South Slopes/Ridge (C2) |
| **31. Longs** (14,259') | Front | Fri–Sat, Aug 5–6 | Keyhole (C3) |
| 32. Pikes (14,111') | Front | Sat–Sun, Aug 6–7 | Pikes Peak Cog Railway (C1) |
| Mount Rainier, WA (14,411') | Cascades | Wed, Aug 10 | Muir/DC Rte (Glaciers, C2+) |
| Mount Rainier, WA (14,411') | Cascades | Wed–Thu, Aug 10–11 | Muir/DC Rte (Glaciers, C2+) |
| **33. Elbert** (14,433') | Sawatch | Sat–Sun, Aug 13–14 | Northeast Ridge (C1) |
| 34. Huron (14,003') | Sawatch | Mon–Tue Aug. 15–16 | Northwest Slopes (C2) |
| 35. Missouri (14,067') | Sawatch | Tue–Wed Aug. 16–17 | Northwest Ridge (C2) |
| 37a. Belford (14,197')** | Sawatch | Wed Aug. 17 | From Elkhead Pass (C1) |
| 36. Oxford (14,153') | Sawatch | Wed–Thu Aug. 17–18 | W. Ridge from Belford (C2) |
| 37b. Belford (14,197') T | Sawatch | Thu Aug. 18 | E. Ridge from Oxford (C2) |
| 37c. Belford (14,197') | Sawatch | Thu–Fri Aug.18–19 | West Slopes (C2 |
| **45b. Capitol** (14,130') *** | Elk | Fri Aug. 19 | Knife Edge–NE Ridge (C4) |
| 38. Snowmass (14,092') | Elk | Mon–Tue Aug. 22–23 | East Slopes–Snowmass (C3) |
| 43a. Little Bear (14,037')*** | Sangre de Cristo | Thu Aug. 25 | West Ridge/Hourglass (C4) |
| 39. Ellingwood Pt. (14,042') | Sangre de Cristo | Thu–Fri Aug. 25–26 | Southwest Face (C2+) |
| 40a. Blanca (14,345') T | Sangre de Cristo | Fri Aug. 26 | Northwest Face (C2) |
| 40b. Blanca (14,345') | Sangre de Cristo | Fri–Sat Aug. 26–27 | Northwest Face (C2) |
| 43b. Little Bear (14,037')*** | Sangre de Cristo | Sat Aug. 27 | Bear Attacks Truck (C4) |
| 41. Lindsey (14,042') | Sangre de Cristo | Mon–Tue Aug. 29–30 | North Face (C2+) |
| 42. Culebra (14,047') | Sangre de Cristo | Wed–Thu Aug. 31–Sept. 1 | Northwest Snake Ridge (C2) |
| **43c. Little Bear** (14,037') | Sangre de Cristo | Fri–Sat Sept. 2–3 | West Ridge/Hourglass (C4) |
| 44a. Shavano (14,229') | Sawatch | Sat–Sun Sept. 3–4 | East Slopes (C2) |
| **45c. Capitol** (14,130') | Elk | Sat–Sun Sept. 10–11 | Knife Edge–NE Ridge (C4) |
| 46. Crestone Peak (14,294') | Sangre de Cristo | Mon–Tue Sept.12–13 | S. Face/Red Col. (C3) |
| 47. Crestone Needle (14,197') | Sangre de Cristo | Tue–Wed Sept. 13–14 | S. Face/Gullies (C3) |
| 48. Humboldt (14,064') | Sangre de Cristo | Wed–Thu Sept. 14–15 | West Ridge (C2) |
| 49a. Challenger (14,081')** X | Sangre de Cristo | Fri Sept. 16 | N. Slopes/E. Ridge (C2+) |
| 50. Kit Carson (14,165') | Sangre de Cristo | Fri–Sat Sept. 16–17 | W. Ridge via Chall. Pt. (C3) |
| 49b. Challenger (14,081') X | Sangre de Cristo | Sat Sept. 17 | From Kit Carson (C3) |
| 44b. Shavano (14,229')** | Sawatch | Sun Sept. 18 | E. Slopes to T–guache (C2) |
| 51. Tabeguache (14,155') | Sawatch | Sun–Mon Sept. 18–19 | SE. Ridge via Shavano (C2) |
| 44c. Shavano (14,229')** | Sawatch | Mon Sept. 19 | N. Ridge from T–guache (C2) |
| 52. Antero (14,269') | Sawatch | Mon–Tue Sept. 19–20 | W. Slopes/Baldwin Gulch (C2) |
| 53. Princeton (14,197') | Sawatch | Tue–Wed Sept. 20–21 | East Slopes (C2) |
| 54. Harvard (14,420') | Sawatch | Wed–Thu Sept. 21–22 | South Slopes (C2) |
| 55. Columbia (14,073') | Sawatch | Thu–Fri Sept. 22–23 | West Face/S. Ridge (C2) |
| 56. Yale (14,196') | Sawatch | Fri–Sat Sept. 23–24 | Southwest Slopes (C2) |
| 57. Massive (14,421') | Sawatch | Mon–Tue Sept. 26–27 | West Slopes/N. Halfmoon (C2) |
| 58. Holy Cross (14,005') | Sawatch | Tue–Wed Sept. 27–28 | Cross Creek/N. Ridge (C2) |

## Totals

| | | |
|---|---|---|
| 73–14,000' Peaks Climbed | All 6 Colorado 14er Mtn. Ranges and Mt. Rainier | 95 Days, 55 Nights above 14,000 feet |

Bold indicates summit bivouacs joined by Chris Tomer.

**Indicates peaks that were climbed in order to get to a summit bivy of a separate fourteener.

***Indicates peaks that were climbed to the top or close to the summit but did not include a summit bivy initially for the project due to inclement weather. The peak had to be done at a later date as a result.

X Indicates peaks that were climbed and not slept on due to "unofficial" fourteener status. A "nap" was taken on these peaks.

OB Indicates peaks where a tent was not set up on the summit, an open overnight bivy was performed.

T Indicates peaks climbed to set up a tent on the summit, then retreated to wait out possible storms and peak re–climbed for sunset.

# Appendix B: Climbing Difficulty Classifications of Colorado's Fourteeners

**Class 1:** Trail hiking or any hiking across open country that is no more difficult than walking on a maintained trail. The parking lot at the trailhead is easy Class 1, groomed ski trails are midrange Class 1, and some of the big step-ups on the rocks near the top of the Barr Trail of Pikes Peak are difficult Class 1.

**Class 2:** Steep trail and/or climber's trail hiking, or off-trail hiking. Class 2 usually means bushwhacking or hiking on a talus or loose rock slope. You are not yet using handholds for upward movement. Occasionally, the rating Class 2+ is used for a pseudo-scrambling route where you will use your hands but do not need to search very hard for handholds. Most people are able to downclimb Class 2+ terrain facing out and without the use of hands, while using superb balance and careful stepping.

**Class 3:** The easiest climbing (not hiking) category. People usually call this "scrambling." You are beginning to look for and use handholds for upward movement. Basic climbing techniques are used, which are noticeably past the level of any walking movements. Although you are using handholds, you don't have to look very hard to find them. Occasionally putting your hand down for balance while crossing a talus slope does not qualify as Class 3. That is still Class 2. About half of the people feel the need to face in toward the rock while downclimbing Class 3.

**Class 4:** This level of climbing is within the realm of "technical climbing." You are not just using handholds; you have to search for, select, and test them. You are beginning to use muscle groups not involved with hiking, those of the upper body and abdominals in particular. Movement at Class 4 is more focused, thoughtful, and slower. Many people prefer to rappel down a serious Class 4 pitch that is exposed rather than to downclimb it. Many Class 3 routes in California would be rated at a Class 4 in Colorado.

**Class 5:** Technical climbing and nothing less. You are now using a variety of climbing techniques, not just cling holds. Movements may involve stemming with your legs, cross-pressure with your arms, pressing down on handholds as you pass them, edging on small holds, smearing, chimneying, jamming, and heel hooks. A lack of flexibility will be noticeable, and can hinder movement, and any movement at Class 5 or above totally occupies the mind of the individual. Most all people choose to rappel down Class 5 pitches.

## Class 5 climbing described using the Yosemite Decimal System Classification

| Class | Description |
|---|---|
| 5.0–5.7 | Easy for experienced climbers; where most climbers begin. Two or three great handholds/footholds are present for upward movement using the four extremities. |
| 5.8–5.9 | Where most weekend climbers become comfortable; employs the specific skills of rock climbing, such as jamming, liebacks, and mantels. One or two good handholds/footholds are present for upward movement using the four extremities. |
| 5.10 | A dedicated weekend climber may attain this level; strong fingers and great footwork necessary, only one good handhold/foothold per four extremities for upward movement. |
| 5.11–5.15 | The realm of true experts; demands much training and natural ability, and often, repeated working of a route utilizing very few handholds of solid grip, many times zero handholds at all four extremities. |

Climbing low Class 5 on the Maroon Bells.

12 x 16 acrylic painting by David Tomer.

# Acknowledgments

We have been fortunate to climb and enjoy Colorado's fourteeners for this project and for many years prior to this endeavor. There are so many people to recognize. Our parents, Bob and Barbara Kedrowski, as well as David and Diane Tomer were tremendous supporters. To Bob and Barb in Vail, thanks for providing a refuge to rest in between summit bivys, and making sure we called to check in. To Diane for all those home-cooked feasts and to David, your acrylic paintings have provided an incredible addition to this book. And, to Megan Fischbach for your love and patience.

Jared Kedrowski provided his motorcycle toward the end of the project, which proved to be a lifesaver accessing Mount Massive. Krista Kedrowski, my sister, and my sister-in-law Michelle, thanks for all your encouragement. Little Kash might want to someday try to repeat this project! I can't forget my brother Robbe and his wife Allison, please enjoy this special journey. Long-time friends of mine in Durango, Bob Pietrack

and his wife Lauren, thanks for a base in the San Juans in between climbs and basketball camps. I also want to dedicate this book to my grandmother, Leona Kedrowski, who will be turning ninety this summer.

For making contributions to this book: Special thanks goes to John Fielder, Colorado's most iconic photographer; and for quotes: Coach Scott Drew, Bob Boeder, Gerry Roach, and Diane Van Daren.

We appreciate the gear sponsorship from Sierra Designs in Boulder, Colorado. The blue tent in many of the shots was an original that Jon purchased in 1994, but fate would have it that a chance meeting on a peak led to testing additional gear, including sleeping bags and pads throughout the project. Thanks to the one and only Rebecca Larsen for setting up the partnership with Eric Larsen, Sue Timbo, Devorah Pearson, and the rest of the gang at American Recreation/Sierra Designs. We look forward to working with you and your team in the future.

The long hours of hard work by the editing/design/sales/marketing team at Westcliffe/Big Earth: Linda Doyle, Mira Perrizo, Rebecca Finkel, and Travis Peterman. We hope you want to entertain our next book.

You guys are awesome! Map design contributions came from Dr. Matthew Novak.

These folks should be considered contributors in some form to the overall project even if they only hiked part of a mountain with us, shot a photo, wrote a story, or even stopped to hear about our endeavor and offer their generosity. You are all still part of the story: Eric George, Jillian Emery, Chuck Schaefer and Kathy Rowberg, Krista Schaefer, Sonja Schaefer, Bobby Hill, Carlos DeLeon, Milton Gonzalez, Brad Siler, Valerie Aragon, Brent and Erin Eskew, Kelly Erikson, Greg Tonagel, Paul Perea, Jennifer Broome, Chris Parente, Jeremy Hubbard, Deborah Takahara, Richard Ortner, Jake Pacheco, Nick Carter, Dave Fraser, Ed Kosowski, Peter Maroney, Benjamin Honigman, KDVR/KWGN-TV, Randy Wyrick, Ryan Grenoble, Tom Wyatt, Torry Udall, Diane Purtz, Trey and Danielle Shelton, Clayton Whitesides, Ty Sterkel, Vince Nethery, Alfred Fresquez, Mandy Hughes, Erik Lambert, Abbey Smith, Luke Bauer, Michael Ahrens, Ned Barr, Bob Hofman, George Boedecker Jr., Morris Ubelacker, Jim Huckabay, Todd Potestio, Phil Cain, and many others we didn't have room to mention here.